How to Beat Satan and Help Others

A Guide for Spiritual Warfare

Kathleen Myers

Copyright

Dedications

To Mike Keep, my teacher, mentor, and friend, definitely puts God first in his life, with his family and friends not far behind. Long ago, he committed his life to serving God, loving his family, and to help those he encountered. Currently, he demonstrates God's love and serves God's people through his Deliverance Ministry - Walking in Freedom Waco. As he leads this ministry, he has and will touch thousands of lives. God has rewarded Mike's steadfast love and devotion by giving Mike the gifts and talents he needs to serve others - the gifts of prophecy, discernment, faith, speaking in tongues, discerning spirits, and knowledge. Because of these gifts, Mike is able to speak directly into the hearts and lives of the people he encounters. Through God, he brings healing, understanding, direction, and comfort into their lives. Mike is a Prophet. Those of us who minister with Mike are blessed to have him in our lives. As God's humble servant and in his humility, Mike has said the same thing about us.

To those of you who have been freed from your own demonic oppression and are now choosing to help others do the same, I dedicate this book. "And these signs will accompany those who believe: In my name they will drive out demons..." *(Mark 16:17)*

In my own life, I am fortunate to have been married to a man who lived every day serving, loving, helping, and guiding others. He showed them how to receive God's love, to turn to Jesus for compassion and wisdom, and to the Holy Spirit for guidance. Even though Terry is with Jesus, his ministry to others is ongoing. Today, those who lived in despair are not, those who lived in fear are not, those who lived in addiction are not, and those who lived in disbelief are not. In their freedom, others are now free. To his memory of service to his Lord, I dedicate this book.

INDEX

Introduction

Let me introduce myself to you. I was baptized as a child and was taught about Jesus in the Methodist Church. My childhood was not perfect, as many are not. My mother had mental health issues. From as early as I can remember, she abused my sisters and me. At that time, I did not know that all of the pain, anger, and disapproval I experienced would have any good purpose in my life. All those terrible experiences taught me how to survive, how to have a passion for Jesus, and how to have compassion for others. Through God, I learned I needed to forgive and not to judge anyone. This took years to do. Eventually, I grew to understand that everything I went through, God was with me and was preparing me for service to others.

My life has been centered on God and Jesus for as long as I can remember. However, it did take me a while to fully understand and appreciate the Holy Spirit. I knew He was there, but did not really understand how the Trinity, God the Father, God the Son, and God the Holy Spirit work together as One. When I understood who God really is to me, I learned God always has a better way, and He walks the walk with me daily. That is when everything changed.

In my early twenties, I became a member of the Episcopal Church. By my mid-twenties, I went to work for an Episcopal Church as a lay professional. During this time, I was a Director of Christian Education and Christian Curriculum writer for children and young people, a Christian Education Teacher for Church volunteers, and a member of a multi-denominational Exorcism Team. As God would have it, over a period of fifteen years He placed me in several different churches as a Christian Education Director, a Director of Lay Ministry, a Co-Director and co-author of a Lay Ministry School for the Dioceses of Arizona, a Seminary Christian Education supervisor, a Christian education and a multi denominational goal setting consultant for leadership and teachers around the country, a

Pastural Counselor and an author of Christian Children books. I had no formal education in Christian Education, Training Teachers to Teach, Pastoral Counseling, Theology, Liturgy, Public Speaking, Goal Setting, writing Curriculum and Books, and Performing Exorcisms (as it was called in those days). Even though I did not have the degrees, I did receive the knowledge and ability I needed from God so that I could complete His callings. What I learned is that God walks with you and guides you throughout your life. If you are willing to listen and to follow Him, God will lead you and give you what you need to do His work in the world.

For about twenty years, God sent me to the world of philanthropy and business. This provided me opportunities to minister to others in a different setting. God had given me ample opportunity to learn about leadership, budgets, goal setting, teaching, counseling, negotiating, raising money, and more. Over the years, I have been the president of a national software corporation, a retail business owner, a cattle rancher, a potbelly pig breeder, an author, and the working president of a philanthropic organization. Amazing, huh? There is no way this could have happened without guidance from God and His divine intervention.

Everything I have ever done in my life prepared me for my next step, even if I did not know what my next step would be. In my early fifties, I became a volunteer in the church. I have been a missionary board member in charge of the missionary houses, a Life Group Leader, an usher, a coordinator for several Church teaching events, a Sunday morning Intercessor, and a Prophetic Prayer Team Coach. Currently, I am a Life Group Leader, a Mentor for young women, and a Deliverance Minister. I can now add to this list the author of books that can help you practice spiritual warfare with confidence, knowledge, and skill.

I have learned from all of this that living anything is possible. If you have faith in God and get out of His way, He will lead you, and miracles happen. Things you thought were never possible are possible, and skills you thought you never had become real. So, here I sit as a sample of what God can do if you just let Him. My favorite Bible verse is *Matthew 8:20*: "Fear not, for I am with you always, even unto the end of the age." So, Fear Not God is with you, no matter what.

Now back to work:

As a disciple of Christ, you will learn how to use your divine authority against evil. You will learn how to recognize and defeat and guard against demonic attacks on yourself, your family, and your friends. Through these books, you will gain exact knowledge about how to defeat Satan and his demons. This includes the attacks that affect you personally, your family, and your friends.

Through the love of God, the power of Jesus Christ, the guidance of the Holy Spirit, and the knowledge in the Bible, you will gain more information and guidance by means of these three books below. You will be able to acquire the information you need to win this war against evil and spiritually strengthen yourself. It is time to embrace the victory God has already won for you. And, for you to learn how to beat Satan and free yourself, your family, and others.

These three books are a trilogy and are designed to build on each other.

Book One

"How To Beat Satan at His Own Game – A Guide for Spiritual Warfare" is written for those of you who are interested in more knowledge about the demonic, how demons operate, and how they are defeated. It is a very practical, educational book that will enable you to defeat demons through the power of God, Jesus, and the Holy Spirit. It provides in-depth instruction about the various aspects of demons, what to do about demonic attack, and how to win your spiritual war by defeating Satan and his demons. It gives you ways to spiritually strengthen yourself so that in the future Satan and his demons cannot enter your physical, emotional, mental, or spiritual life.

Book Two

"How to Beat Satan and Free Your Family – A Parent's Guide for Spiritual Warfare" is written to enable you as a parent to learn how to join hands with Jesus as you enter and defeat the ongoing demonic war against you and your family. It is geared to parents of children from birth through the teen years. Filled with Biblical Scriptures and specific instructions, this book gives you knowledge about how to fight back in many areas of your family's life, including the occult, The information in this book will help you recognize demonic influence so that you can fight and win these demonic battles. Also, how you can fight back through the Deliverance Ministry and Baptism.

Book Three

"How To Beat Satan and Help Others" – A Guide for Spiritual Warfare is written for those of you who are interested in more knowledge about how to identify, ward off, and overcome demonic influence. This instructional book includes topics such as what demons are, how demons attack, how demons work together, and how demons use demonic groups, churches, and organizations. It also teaches you how to identify and respond to the demonic, how to ward off demons, and how to respond to demonic attack. How to Beat Satan and Help Others includes an outline of an informational model for Deliverance Ministry.

The Bible is clear about Satan and his demons being active in this world. The following are a few of the approximately 21 verses in the New Testament that directly mention demons. There are also approximately 49 other verses and 56 mentions of Satan and his demons.

Since I am a teacher at heart, it is hard for me not to teach. Therefore, Bible verses are used throughout all three books to verify that the content of each book is biblically based.

Ephesians 6:11-13

"Put on the full armor of God, so that you can take your stand against the devil's schemes. For our struggle is not against flesh and blood, but against the rulers, against the authorities, against the powers of this dark world and against the spiritual forces of evil in the heavenly realms. Therefore, put on the full armor of God, so that when the day of evil comes, you may be able to stand your ground, and after you have done everything, to stand."

James 4:7

"Submit yourselves, then, to God. Resist the devil, and he will flee from you."

1 Peter 5:8-9

Be alert and of sober mind. Your enemy the devil prowls around like a roaring lion looking for someone to devour. Resist him, standing firm in the faith, because you know that the family of believers throughout the world is undergoing the same kind of sufferings.

Romans 8:37-39

"No, in all these things we are more than conquerors through him who loved us. For I am convinced that neither death nor life, neither angels nor demons,[a] neither the present nor the future, nor any powers,[39] neither height nor depth, nor anything else in all creation, will be able to separate us from the love of God that is in Christ Jesus our Lord."

Jesus gave us authority, as His disciples, to conquer Satan and to help those who are in demonic bondage. We, as believers in Christ and servants to His people, and through the love of God, the powerful name of Jesus Christ, and the wisdom and guidance of the Holy Spirit, can defeat Satan and his demons. God is on our side.

Read, study, and prepare yourself. Then turn to Him for direction. In His infinite wisdom and great love for us, God has given us all the tools we need to take on Satan's demons and win the battles. Through the power in the name of Jesus Christ and the wisdom and guidance of the Holy Spirit, we can fight these battles without fear. This book is written for the purpose of teaching you and your family how to enter into spiritual warfare and beat Satan and his demons at their own game. It can mean freedom for those you help to become who God means for them to be. All they have to do is say "Yes to Jesus - they just have to want it.

I will be praying for you as you move forward in your walk with God. May He direct and protect you and those you love. Remember: "Fear not for I am with you even until the end of the age." Amen

Explanation of Demons

The fall of angels in the Bible refers to a rebellion led by Satan, where he and some of his angels were cast out of heaven. This expulsion is a central theme in some biblical interpretations, with verses in Isaiah and Ezekiel describing Satan's pride and fall, and Revelation depicting a war in heaven. Angels were cast out of heaven for rebelling against God, an act of pride led by Satan, who sought to be equal to or greater than God. The rebellion involved a portion of the angels who chose to follow Satan's lead instead of God's authority. As a result, they were expelled from heaven and became what are known as fallen angels or demons

The exact time of the angels' fall from heaven is not known, but biblical interpretations place the event after the creation of angels and before the temptation of Adam and Eve, meaning it occurred sometime after creation and before Genesis Chapter 3. Jesus also mentioned this fall. *(Luke 10:18)*, "I saw Satan fall like lightning from heaven," an event he witnessed firsthand.

They were cast out of Heaven by God and are now known on Earth as demons. They are spiritual beings and do not have physical bodies. They do not live, grow old, and die like human beings, but exist in a spiritual state. Because of this, they have significant power and influence in this world. They are completely fallen, desperately evil to the core, and in the service of their supreme ruler. Although not nearly to the extent of the almighty Creator God, who rules over them. Satan and all of his demons are now under the judgment of God, which occurs at the final judgment when they are cast into the lake of fire.

According to the Bible, the very spirit of demons is evil. While we do not know when their rebellion against God occurred, we do know that demons are now completely fallen, desperately evil, and in the service of the supreme ruler of Hell, Satan. His primary goals are to lure all of mankind, including children, away from God through sin and lies, causing them to doubt their faith, and ultimately separating them from God for all eternity. Satan uses temptation, accusation, and deceit to thwart God's plan. All of Satan's demons are dedicated to following Satan's mission by seeking to corrupt humanity and by destroying as much of God's creation as possible.

As a believer in Jesus, who is Baptized in His name, you can be confident and secure in the power of Jesus Christ and in the presence of the Holy Spirit within you. You cannot be possessed, but you can be oppressed, negatively influenced by Demons. According to the Bible, our goal is to think rightly about these evil spiritual beings—especially their ultimate fear is the name of Jesus Christ. "You believe that there is one God. Good! Even the demons believe that—and shudder." *(James 2:19)*

At the Second Coming, the Bible confirms that Satan will be chained in the abyss for a thousand years *(Revelation 20:1-3)*. Christ went to the Abyss. *(Romans 10:7)* The abyss is described as a prison for demons and Satan, while they await God's Final Judgment. After the Final Judgment they will never be free to go out and disturb God's creation. *(Luke 8:31) (2 Peter 2:4).*

Mission of Demons

Demons are all evil to the core. They try to kill, steal, and destroy as much of mankind as possible and ruin God's creation by using these methods.

Temptation

Demons are tempters, luring you into wrongdoing through deception and manipulation.

Attacks on Faith

Causing people to abandon their faith, commit heresy, or turn away from God.

Chaos and Destruction

Demon's actions result in disruption, chaos, and harm to you, your children, and society.

Opposition to Goodness

They want to turn all of mankind away from God. They want to lead all humans away from the true Gospel of Jesus Christ and God's purpose in your life. They want to hinder your spiritual growth and your connection with God. They are intent on destroying God's plan and purpose for you and your children.

Possession

Demons can take control of your body and mind, potentially leading to symptoms like seizures, physical violence, or a loss of speech or sight,

Satan and his demons are attacking adults and children. *(Mark 7:15-20, Luke 9:37-42, Matthew 15:21-28)* Demons use all means available to separate you and your children from God. They absolutely want the worst for your family. They want to influence you and your children's interests and passions to the point that the family is broken. The closer they get to your children, the more demons interact with them and the more they try to destroy them. They do not want you to achieve God's purpose in your life. In some of the most destructive ways possible, demons can lead you and your children into sin, destruction, and in some cases, death.

One method they use is through demonic oppression, which is demonic influence over of your mind, body, and emotions. Symptoms can range from a general lack of motivation and joy to specific behaviors or thoughts that are contrary to God's character. Remember, even though you believe in Jesus Christ, you can still be oppressed in these ways and more. Demons achieve their purpose through your sins, bad choices, and generational curses. Each one of these opens doors for Satan and his demons to enter your life.

Demonic Oppression can manifest as:

- A lack of interest in spiritual activities
- Difficulty in prayer
- Persistent negative thoughts and emotions
- Disobedience
- Decline in health and relationship with friends and family
- Nightmares
- Trouble sleeping

Demonic Possession can dramatically influence different aspects of life. You can be possessed due to spiritual weakness and sin, which makes you more susceptible to demonic attack.

In the worst-case scenarios, it can take over your mind, body, emotions, and soul. Your life can turn from light to darkness, good to bad, and joy to fear. Possession examples follow below.

Demonic Possession manifests as:

- Hallucinations, strange behavior, extreme unrest, changes in voice, speaking in foreign languages, seizures, and superhuman strength.
- Personality shifts, violence, and self-mutilation
- Superhuman strength, physical pain, and a change in voice are among the physical manifestations attributed to demonic possession.

A non-believer and/or an unbaptized person, no matter what their age, will find it much harder to guard against and to fight off evil. When you and your children proclaim Jesus as Lord and Savior and are baptized in His name, you can be confident and secure in the power of Jesus Christ. With the presence of the Holy Spirit dwelling within you and your children, you can be sure of help, guidance, and protection from demonic attack. "A scoundrel plots evil, and on their lips it is like a scorching fire. A perverse person stirs up conflict, and a gossip separates close friends. A violent person entices their neighbor and leads them down a path that is not good." *(Proverbs 16:27-29).*

Demon's Legal Rights

The progress of Deliverance is often dependent on four main parts:

- Removing legal rights
- Tearing down strongholds
- Casting out the remaining demons

There are other parts that also influence the progress of Deliverance. If you try to cast out demons without taking away the strongholds or legal rights that they are holding onto, you will not be as successful. Removing all of these, plus potentially others, is vital in a complete and successful Deliverance.

Legal Rights

A legal right is something that can give demons an opportunity to enter or harass you, or give them the right to remain in you, even when you try to cast them out. Some of the most common legal rights that are faced when ministering deliverance are:

Sins

When you commit sin, it gives the enemy a legal right to affect or bother you in numerous ways. As an example, when you allow unholy thoughts to enter your mind, it can open the door to a demon. Ignoring this sin will eventually cause you to commit more sins. It starts when demons persuade you to think the wrong thought. When you accept it and you make it a bad habit, it opens the door for the demons to move in further. If you continue down this path, you will continue to open more doors for Satan and his demons. Eventually, this will lead you to more sinning, such as lying, stealing, committing adultery, rape, and many more. Once these sins are committed, more doors are opened. The feelings and desires that the demons continue to push on you are irresistible. It is like a snowball going down the hill. Sin opens the door to demons, which pushes you in the direction of more sins, which then opens the door wider to more demons, and on and on.

The answer to this is repentance. Verbally confess and repent of your sins that have given the demons legal rights in your life. If you recognize a particular sin or sins that have opened the door to the oppression you are experiencing and are seeking deliverance from, you need to repent of the sins that caused the bondage. Any larger or gross sins you can remember, it is always good to repent of them specifically. Repentance is very important in Deliverance. If you do not confess your sins and try to hide them from others, and if you do not repent of these sins to Jesus, it leaves that sin in your life, causing havoc and pain. You have to confess our sins in order to be forgiven "If we confess our sins, he is faithful and just and will forgive us our sins and purify us from all unrighteousness." *(1 John 1-9).*

Types Of Sin

Soul Ties

Repentance, renunciation, and breaking of soul ties are important. First, definitely repent of the sin that caused the soul tie to be formed. Then use your authority through Jesus Christ to break and sever the unholy soul tie. Repentance and the breaking of soul ties in Jesus' name is the way you can solve this problem.

Demonic Oaths and Vows

A demonic vow can be like a spiritual signature that demons use as a legal right to gain access into your life. Demonic vows can be made consciously or unconsciously. Often, if you join a cult, a Satanist, a Coven, and even some organizations like secret societies that use secret passwords, initiation rituals, oaths, and loyalty unto death. Blood oath covenants, Theistic Satanic groups, Satanists, The Illuminati, role-playing occult games like Dungeons and Dragons, etc. You can be required to make vows with Satan, which you may not realize you are doing. This gives the demon legal right to be in your life. Demonic vows can be made unconsciously just by dabbling with the occult, even just curious about the occult, and reading forbidden materials, which include horoscopes, Eight Balls, and Tarot Cards, tells demons that you are interested in them. The only vows that are practical and good are those made in the name of Jesus, such as weddings, Baptism, Vows to God, etc. If you have made vows that do not glorify God, then you need to repent and renounce those vows verbally and seek God's forgiveness.

Forgiveness

If there is any bitterness involved, such as someone who caused you a traumatic experience and you are still holding it against them, then you must forgive the person who hurt you. Repent for holding onto the bitterness in your heart towards them. When we do not forgive others, God does not forgive us. "For if you do not forgive others, God will not forgive your sins." *(Matthew 6:14-15)*. Another example is The Parable of the Unforgiving Servant *(Matthew 18:21-35)*. When God does not forgive us, it leaves our sins remaining, which can give demons legal rights in our lives. The legal ground the enemy may be standing on to torment you it may very well be rooted in unforgiveness. Forgiveness is not an option; it is a necessity. It is the key to our relationship with God. So, repent for holding bitterness in your heart against others and make a solid choice to forgive those who have wronged you. Confirm your choice of forgiveness by verbally forgiving others. This releases the bitterness and hurt from your heart against others. Forgiveness is an act of Grace, just as God forgave us through Jesus Christ.

Generational Curses

Generational Curses can produce negative traits and behavior, especially dysfunctional behaviors. Adversities in your life can be passed down through a family's lines from one generation to the next. They are rooted in sin or trauma. The experiences of our ancestors can create a negative legacy and impact subsequent generations. These cures are not necessarily your fault. When you break generational curses, you are breaking these curses for your children and future generations. Generational Curses can often be seen passed down family bloodlines through addiction, adultery, physical and emotional abuse, lack of faith in God, and other sins. Generational Curses are very common in families.

Childhood Rejection

Much demonic bondage is caused during childhood. For example, if you showed rejection towards your child, a demon of rejection may enter. If you have been rejected by either your parents or anyone else, the demon of rejection is usually present in these situations and should be cast out. To completely overcome this rejection, you must make a solid choice to forgive the person(s) who hurt you. You can release the hurt in your heart against them and give it to God.

Points of Weakness

When you experience weakness, such as emotional shock, physical trauma, fearful experiences during childhood, and other areas. The natural wall of defense and the physical, spiritual, or emotional system of a person is weakened. It leaves you vulnerable for Satan to attach himself to you. The same is true with drinking excessive amounts of alcohol, sexual addiction, and using drugs. Drugs, alcohol, or any other addiction lowers your defenses. Since demons thrive on weakness, they love to move right in and begin to deceive you. This can pull you farther away from God.

Spoken Self-Curses

The words we say have spiritual value. The Bible says to bless and not curse, and that the tongue has the power of life and death. If you walk around saying, "I wish I could just die," a demon may hear you and then push you closer to death through the power of their lies. If this is the case, renounce what you said or thought against yourself. Then, as a child of God, repent for thinking and speaking such things. Ask God for forgiveness, and then you must forgive yourself for your shortcomings. Say, "In the name of Jesus Christ, I break all curses I have spoken against myself, and I put it under the blood of Jesus." You can repeat this as many times as you like.

Cursed Objects

Physical objects can carry demonic influence, such as idols, occult books, rings, movies, charms, etc. If you have brought any Indian or pagan religious artifacts and any Occult items into your home, repent and destroy all of these. They are open doors for demonic intrusion and oppression for the people living in your home. Burn or destroy any objects you have located that can be of Satan or of pagan followers. *(Isaiah 2:18)*, "And the idols he shall utterly abolish." It is Biblical to burn cursed objects. Land can also become defiled by the sins of its owners. "...for all these things were done by the people who lived in the land before you, and the land became defiled.

(Leviticus 18:27). Your home and our property can be cleansed by prayer and repentance of the sins of the previous owners.

Renounce Demons

Renounce any known demons that have been invited through spirit guides, seances, demonic rituals, and any interest or involvement in the occult - Witchcraft, Satanism, etc. Also, renounce any demons that you know need to be cast out. This explains to the demons that you are no longer interested in having them around and that you are taking measures to cast them out.

Other Helpful Things To Look For

Try to identify how the negative or unholy problem started and what gave the demons the ability to enter. Look for any involvement in the occult, sins, vows, traumatic experiences, etc., along with any unusual happenings - emotionally, mentally, or physically.

Demonic Attack

As we know, demons attack people in order to oppose God's purposes and to deceive God's people in any way they can. Demons can attack you through various means, including tempting you to sin, causing physical ailments, and influencing your thoughts, feelings, and behaviors. They seek to destroy your faith, relationships, and overall well-being.

Demons use a variety of tactics to deceive, oppress, and ultimately hinder people from following God. These tactics are used to control and discourage you, so that you will turn away from God.

Deception

Paul warns Timothy about false teachings that are opposed to the Gospel. Paul does not stop at simply identifying these teachings as false; he says that people who believe false things about Jesus are following the "teachings of demons". *(1 Timothy 4:1-3)*. This makes sense because demons are in the service of Satan, who is the father of lies and the king of deceit.

False Religions

The Bible seems to suggest that demonic influence actually lies behind false religions, any belief that opposes the Gospel of Jesus Christ, the Son of God. The first commandment, "You shall have no other gods before Me," *(Exodus 20:3-6)*. The prohibition against making idols, bowing down to them, or serving them is definitely a warning against false religions. People who question or reject Jesus have not just chosen a different religion; they are actually deceived by Satan and are unknowingly serving him and his demons. Every man or woman either believes in Jesus as the Son of God or believes some form of the teachings of demons, which are through sins, lies, and deceit.

Possession

Demons can take control of our bodies, minds, and emotions. This is when demons exert control over a person's actions and thoughts. While the exact phrases "demonic possession or oppression" or "Deliverance" are not used, many accounts in the Bible do describe people being "possessed" by demons,

The goal of possession is total destruction of the person being possessed. *(Mark 5:1-13)*. The demons' goal is to steal souls from God. As an example, after Jesus ordered demons to leave the body of the person, He decided to send the demons into the pigs. The pigs then ran off a cliff and died. Only the power of Jesus could conquer and control the demons trying to steal the man's life. Demons are able to possess only those who have not been Baptized and do not profess Jesus as their Lord and Savior. Because of this, these people are exposed to the possibility of complete demonic control over their lives.

Oppression

It is important to note the Bible does not suggest that demons are able to possess Christians who have faith in Jesus Christ as Lord and Savior. Those who have been Baptized and have faith in Jesus have the Holy Spirit living within them. "Therefore put on the full armor of God, so that when the day of evil comes, you may be able to stand your ground, and after you have done everything, to stand." *(Ephesians 6:13)*. Demons cannot coexist with the Holy Spirit. Even though baptized and believers in Jesus, Christians cannot be possessed. They can be influenced to sin and to do evil by the demonic attacks in your mind, body, and emotions. This is called demonic oppression.

Manipulation

Demons may subtly guide you towards destructive behaviors and choices, often appealing to your desires and vulnerabilities. This is true for all people. This can involve tempting you with earthly possessions, pleasures, or power. They can blind unbelievers and persuade some Christians to ignore the gospel. They can empower other religions and practices that oppose Christianity. "And even if our gospel is veiled, it is veiled to those who are perishing." The god of this age has blinded the minds of unbelievers, so that they cannot see the light of the gospel that displays the glory of Christ, who is the image of God." *(2 Corinthians 4:34)*

Fear and Intimidation

Demons can use fear and intimidation to control and discourage you from seeking God or embracing your faith. This can involve creating a sense of powerlessness or vulnerability. "God has not given us a spirit of fear but of power, love and of a sound mind." *(2 Timothy 1:7).* The total opposite of an intimidated spirit. When you are fearful and intimidated, it is a scheme of Satan and not of God.

Promoting Evil

Demons are often associated with causing harm, suffering, and chaos in the world, both physically, mentally, and spiritually. The Bible describes demons as spiritual beings who actively seek to attack and influence the world through possession of Christians. These attacks can take various forms, including suffering, deception, and temptation. Demons' goals are to hinder God's purposes and His people. In His sovereign plan, God has allowed the influence of Satan and his demons to continue in this world until the day of his final judgment by Jesus.

For Christian believers, "Put on the full armor of God, so that you can take your stand against Satan's schemes. For our struggle is not against flesh and blood, but against the rulers, against the authorities, against the powers of this dark world and against the spiritual forces of evil in heavenly realms." *(Ephesians 6:10-12).*

Doubt and Discouragement

Demons can sow seeds of doubt and discouragement, making it harder for you to believe in yourself or in your faith. They may try to make you feel unworthy or hopeless. "For I am that neither death nor life, neither angels nor demons, neither the present nor the future, nor any powers, neither height nor depth, nor anything else in all creation, will be able to separate us from the love of God that is in Christ Jesus our Lord." *(Romans 8:38-39).*

Pride and Self-Reliance

Demons can encourage pride and self-reliance, leading you to believe you do not need God or His guidance. This can manifest as a resistance to humility and a rejection of God's authority. "A man's pride will bring him low, but a humble spirit will obtain honor." *(Proverbs 29:23).*

Division and Hatred

Demons can incite division and animosity within communities, particularly within the church. They can exploit conflicts and misunderstandings to weaken the unity of believers. Be sure, watch out, and avoid those who cause divisions and create obstacles contrary to the doctrine that you have been taught. "I urge you, brothers and sisters, to watch out for those who cause divisions and put obstacles in your way that are contrary to the teaching you have learned." *(Romans 16:17).*

Attacks on Faith and Hope

Demons will try to erode your faith and hope, making it harder for you to persevere in the face of adversity. They may attack your sense of purpose and meaning in life. "You believe that there is one God; you do well. Even the demons believe and shudder!" *(James 2:19).*

Exploitation of Vulnerabilities

Demons often seek to exploit vulnerabilities in your life, such as past hurts, unresolved issues, or unmet needs. This can involve targeting areas where you are most susceptible to their influence. "For certain individuals whose condemnation was written about long ago have secretly slipped in among you. They are ungodly people, who pervert the grace of our God into a license for immorality and deny Jesus Christ our only Sovereign and Lord." *(Jude 1:4)*.

Use of Temptation

Demons may use various forms of temptation to lure you away from God, such as tempting you with material wealth, pleasures, or power. This can involve appealing to your desires and vulnerabilities. When tempted, you can say, "God is tempting me." God cannot be tempted by evil, nor does He tempt anyone. *(James 1:4)*.

Encouragement of Idolatry

Demons may encourage idolatry by promoting the worship of false gods or the pursuit of worldly idols. This can involve diverting your attention and allegiance from God to other things. "No, but the sacrifices of pagans are offered to demons, not to God, and I do not want you to be participants with demons. You cannot drink the cup of the Lord and the cup of demons too; you cannot have a part in both the Lord's table and the table of demons." *(1 Corinthians 10:20-20)*.

Use of False Teachers and Teachings

Demons may utilize false teachers and teachings to deceive you and lead you away from the truth. This can involve spreading misinformation, promoting false doctrines, and twisting God's Word. This states that false doctrines have a demonic origin: "in later times some will depart from the faith, giving heed to deceiving spirits and to doctrines of demons". *(1 Timothy 4:1-2).*

Christian Response to The Demonic

Demons are bent on destruction. Because the demons are fallen and evil, they are under the judgment of God. Jesus Christ will finally judge all evil, including the evil of Satan and his demons. They will be thrown into the lake of fire forever. *(Revelations 20:7-10).*

How can you guard yourself against their attacks? What is your ultimate hope in the midst of real spiritual warfare and demonic activity?

- Read and study what the Bible has to say about demons and the spiritual world.

- Acknowledge that the struggle is real and intense. You are engaged in a struggle that is bigger than flesh and blood.

- God claims every part of this world as His. Satan and his demons oppose God's work at every step.

- The work of demonic powers is constant, and it is important that you do not act as if this work does not exist. You need to be aware of the demons' deception.

- It is good for Christians to be on guard against the lies of Satan and his demons. John calls believers to test the spirits: "Beloved, do not believe every spirit, but test the spirits to see whether they are from God, for many false prophets have gone out into the world." *(1 John 4:1).* Deception is one of their primary functions of Satan. Demons delight in deceiving people with words and teachings that are opposed to the life-giving word of Jesus Christ.

- Jesus Christ is the Son of God sent to be the Savior of all who believe. By turning them away from Jesus, Demons are constantly pursuing the deception and destruction of all mankind. So, you need to be watchful and rely on God's love and power.

- You need to remember Jesus's power. John's warning to Christians is about testing the spirits. "He who is in you is greater than He who is in the world." *(1 John 4:4)*.

- Following Jesus Christ and the Holy Spirit dwelling in you, His power and might far outweigh that of the most powerful demon, even Satan himself. Jesus can kill the efforts of Satan and his demons with just a word. His power makes these evil spirits terrified. While we need to acknowledge the power of evil in the world, we should never think it compares to the power of Jesus Christ, the risen Lord.

As you consider the demons' works, their lies, evil, and attacks in this world, you can take comfort in the fact that there will be the final Judgment. Jesus will return to this earth as the Judge and will make all things right. Satan and his demons will be lost, and all the victories are for Jesus.

Meet Daily With God

"For our struggle is not against flesh and blood, but against the rulers, against the authorities, against the powers of this dark world, and against the spiritual forces of evil in the heavenly realms. Therefore put on the full armor of God, so that when the day of evil comes, you may be able to stand your ground, and after you have done everything, to stand. Stand firm then, with the belt of truth buckled around your waist, with the breastplate of righteousness in place, and with your feet fitted with the readiness that comes from the gospel of peace. In addition to all this, take up the shield of faith, with which you can extinguish all the flaming arrows of the evil one. Take the helmet of salvation and the sword of the Spirit, which is the word of God." *(Ephesians 6:12).*

Renounce Any Lies

Write down any lies that you are believing,

Father, are there any lies I believe about You or myself?

Father I renounce the Lie that You are_____ or I am_____

Repent And Commit

"If my people, who are called by my name, will humble themselves and pray and seek my face and turn from their wicked ways, then I will hear from heaven, and I will forgive their sin and will heal their land." *(2 Chronicles 7:14).*

Father, forgive me for partnering with the Enemy and believing his lie _____

Father I commit to You not to walk in the steps of Satan.

Be Forgiven - Rely On God's Mercy And Grace

"All the prophets testify about Him that everyone who believes in Him receives forgiveness of sins through His name." *(Acts 10:41).*

Father, I receive your great forgiveness for my life and I accept your mercy today. I forgive myself for falling short of Your plans for me, as I continue to follow You, daily. Amen.

Be Grateful

"Do not be anxious about anything, but in every situation, by prayer and petition, with thanksgiving, present your requests to God." *(Philippians 4:6).*

Father, what truth do you have for my heart? I exchange any lies for the mercy and love you have shown to me. Amen.

Be Transformed

"Do not conform to the pattern of this world, but be transformed by the renewing of your mind. Then you will be able to test and approve what God's will is—his good, pleasing and perfect will." *(Romans 12:2).*

"Whoever belongs to God hears what God says. The reason you do not hear is that you do not belong to God." *(John 8:47).*

Father. I ask you for the power and strength to follow your will in my life. Amen

Walk In The Spirit

"So I say, walk by the Spirit, and you will not gratify the desires of the flesh." *(Galatians 5:16).*

Renewing your minds and walking in the Spirit, so that beauty can be manifest.

Father, I ask You to help me know Your purpose for my life. Not just what I think You want me to do, but how I can serve You better. Amen.

Meet With God Through Prayer and Scripture

Meeting God daily through the Bible and prayer is critically important for your spiritual life. This involves both listening to God's word and responding to Him in prayer.

This provides a relationship of conversation and connection. It allows God to speak to you through the Bible. You can pause and reflect on His words and then respond to Him in prayer with your own words, praising, thanking, and confessing. To meet with God is not only to hear His words in the Bible. It is also to personally speak to Him directly in prayer.

God speaks to you through the Bible. You listen carefully, as you take it all in. Many times, you speak to Him through your thoughts and feelings. This leads to responding to God with your own words of praise, thankfulness, confession, and prayer. God wants to hear back from you, so you can begin having a conversation with Him.

Prepare Your Heart

Dedicate a specific time and place daily just for God. This is a time to just focus on Him. You

can do this in a variety of ways, such as sitting quietly listening to music, simply sitting still as you separate yourself from your daily life, and reading the Bible. Some people find their quiet space with God in nature, some in prayer, some in meditation, and some in music. No matter what the best way is for you, a regular time and place to meet with God is important.

Ask God to reveal Himself to you and help you hear His voice more clearly. Some people hear Him through the Bible, through music, through discernment, through dreams, and through prayers. Whatever way is best for you is the right way. God is waiting to hear from you, no matter how you do it.

Speaking to God

It is not hard to speak to God. He is always there waiting for you to turn to Him. He has given you many ways to speak to Him. In prayer, you can pray using your own words or the prayers of others. With music, you can relax and wait for the conversation to start. In nature, you can sit quietly and take in the world He created for you. There are many other ways to talk with God. Any way you choose is the right way. God is always waiting for a conversation with you.

- Jesus emphasized talking to God directly and privately.
- Jesus taught the Lord's Prayer as a model, encouraging us to address God as Father, and to ask for our daily needs, forgiveness, and protection from temptation.
- Jesus emphasized the importance of praying in private, rather than for the sake of being seen by others. He stressed the importance of seeking God's will and not simply asking for what we want.
- Jesus taught that prayers should be offered in faith, believing that God will hear and answer.
- Jesus emphasized the reward of those who hear God's word and obey it.
- Jesus highlighted the importance of seeking God's will and the reward for you if you listen to and obey His word.

You can hear from God through His Word, through leading from the Holy Spirit, through prayer, and many other ways. If you are unaware, too distracted, or are just not being attentive to His voice, you can miss it. Remember, prayer is simply your conversation with God. A conversation is a two-way street. Hearing from God is sometimes understood as discerning His guidance and will in your life, not necessarily through audible voices. It is believed that God speaks to those who are seeking Him, living in accordance with His teachings, praising Him, worshiping Him, thanking Him, and reaching out to Him when you need His help to overcome darkness. He is always present in your life, so there are no limits to the ways you can talk to Him or what the conversations will be about.

There are certainly times God reaches out to you, and sometimes you are not paying attention. It is important to think that talking to God is like talking to someone who truly wants the best for you and loves you deeply. It is important to remember that your faith in Him and willingness to follow His guidance allow you to build a strong and important communication with Him. Being humble and open to God's wisdom and the incorporation of all He has to say to you makes your life better. Hearing from God is a process of cultivating a relationship with Him, actively seeking His guidance, and listening to Him for guidance. He is always waiting to talk to us; we just need to listen and respond.

In Humility

Write down any lies that you are believing that separate you from God.

Renounce

Father, are there any lies I believe about You, others, and myself?

> Father,
>
> I renounce _____, the lies I have thought about You.
>
> I renounce _____, the lies I have thought about others.
>
> I renounce _____, the lies I have thought about myself.

Repent

"If my people, who are called by my name, will humble themselves and pray and seek my face and turn from their wicked ways, then I will hear from heaven, and I will forgive their sin and will heal their land." *(2 Chronicles 7:14).*

Father, forgive me for partnering with Satan and believing his lies about You.

Father, forgive me for partnering with Satan and believing his lies about others.

Father, forgive me for partnering with Satan and believing his lies about myself.

Pray

Father, give me the wisdom not to believe his lies and give me the strength to turn only to You for guidance in my life. You are the truth, the way, and the light. Amen

Rely On God's Mercy, Grace, and Power

"All the prophets testify about him that everyone who believes in Him receives His forgiveness of sins through His name." *(Acts 10:41)*.

Receive Forgiveness

Father, I receive your great forgiveness for my life. Because You have forgiven me, I can forgive myself.

Be Grateful

"Give thanks in every circumstance; for this is God's will for you in Christ Jesus." *(1 Thessalonians 5:18)*.

Father, I am grateful for Your love for me, even though I fall short.

Father, I am grateful for Your great love for me

Father, I am grateful You are always there for me in times of trial and times of happiness.

Father, I am grateful that You guide and direct me as I love and serve others. Amen.

Be Transformed

"Do not conform to the pattern of this world, but be transformed by the renewing of your mind. Then you will be able to test and approve what God's will is—his good, pleasing and perfect will." *(Romans 12:2).*

"Whoever belongs to God hears what God says. The reason you do not hear is that you do not belong to God." *(John 8:47).*

Armor Of God

The Armor of God is given to us so that we can resist the Evil One.

James 1:21, "Therefore, put away all filthiness and rampant wickedness and receive with meekness the implanted word, which is able to save your souls."

James 4:7, "Submit yourselves therefore to God. Resist the devil, and he will flee from you."

How To Put On The Armor of God

You "put on" the Armor of God through prayer and intentional focus on the attributes and principles listed below. This involves consciously aligning your thoughts, attitudes, and actions in your daily life with these spiritual principles and relying on God's strength to help you live according to them. Regular prayer, study of the Bible, and fellowship with other believers are vital to this process. Never take your Armor off.

- Finding God by reading scripture and through prayer keeps our minds on God and not on worldly things.
- Trust God knows what is best for me.
- Be thankful for what I have been through because they changed me for the better.

The Armor Of God

"Finally, be strong in the Lord and in his mighty power. Put on the full armor of God, so that you can take your stand against the devil's schemes. For our struggle is not against flesh and blood, but against the rulers, against the authorities, against the powers of this dark world and against the spiritual forces of evil in the heavenly realms. Therefore, put on the full armor of God, so that when the day of evil comes, you may be able to stand your ground, and after you have done everything, to stand. Stand firm then," *(Ephesians 6:10-17).*

The Belt Of Truth

Fasten the belt standing in God's truth. Identify the lies you are believing.

"Therefore, my beloved brethren whom I long to see, my joy and crown, in this way stand firm in the Lord, my beloved." *(Philippians 4:1)*.

"See to it that no one takes you captive by philosophy and empty deceit, according to human tradition, according to the elemental spirits of the world, and not according to Christ." *(Colossians 2:8)*.

"For the weapons of our warfare are not of the flesh but have divine power to destroy strongholds. We destroy arguments and every lofty opinion raised against the knowledge of God, and take every thought captive to obey Christ." *(2 Corinthians 10:4-5)*.

"I have been crucified with Christ. It is no longer I who live, but Christ who lives in me. And the life I now live in the flesh I live by faith in the Son of God, who loved me and   gave himself for me." *(Galatians 2:20)*.

The Sword Of The Spirit

As an offensive and defensive weapon belonging to the Holy Spirit, all Christian soldiers need the same rigid training to properly handle the Sword of the Spirit, "which is the word of God" *(2 Timothy 3:16-17)*.

"All Scripture is God-breathed and is useful for teaching, rebuking, correcting and training in righteousness, so that the servant of God may be thoroughly equipped for every good work. *(2 Corinthians 10:4-5)*.

"For the weapons of our warfare are not of the flesh but have divine power to destroy strongholds. We destroy arguments and every lofty opinion raised against the knowledge of God, and take every thought captive to obey Christ," *(Hebrews 4:12)*.

"For the word of God is living and active, sharper than any two-edged sword, piercing to the division of soul and of spirit, of joints and of marrow, and discerning the thoughts and Intentions of the heart." *(Psalms 11:11)*.

"Teach me, Lord, the way of your decrees, that I may follow it to the end. Give me understanding, so that I may keep your law and obey it with all my heart. Direct me in the path of your commands, for there I find delight. Turn my heart toward your statutes and not toward selfish gain. Turn my eyes away from worthless things; preserve my life according to your word. Fulfill your promise to our servant, so that you may be feared. Take away the disgrace I dread, for your laws are good. How I long for your precepts! In your righteousness preserve my life. *(Psalms 119:33-40)*.

Breastplate Of Righteousness

The Breastplate of Righteousness, in the context of biblical armor, signifies the protection afforded by righteousness from the temptations of the world. It shields our hearts and minds from the "fiery darts of the evil one" *(Ephesians 6:16)*.

"and be found in him, not having a righteousness of my own that comes from the law, but that which is through faith in Christ—the righteousness that comes from God on the basis of faith." *(Philippians 3:9)*.

"But if we walk in the light, as he is in the light, we have fellowship with one another,   and the blood of Jesus his Son cleanses us from all sin." *(1 John 1:17)*.

"If we confess our sins, he is faithful and just and will forgive us our sins and purify us from all unrighteousness." *(1 John 1:9)*.

Shoes Of Peace

The Shoes of Peace provides readiness and preparation that Christians have for sharing the good news of Jesus. We stand firm in faith, as described in *Ephesians 6:15*. This "readiness" is also about being ready to act on it in all areas of life, including spiritual battles and everyday challenges.

"And let the peace of God rule in your hearts, to which also you were called in one body; and be thankful." *(Colossians 3:15)*.

"what you have learned and received and heard and seen in me – practice these things, and the God of Peace will be with you" *(Philippians 4:9)*.

Shield Of Faith

The Shield of Faith is protection from spiritual attack, can extinguish all the flaming arrows of evil, and throw the enemy off guard.

"Be sober-minded; be watchful. Your adversary the devil prowls around like a roaring lion, seeking someone to devour. Resist him, firm in your faith, knowing that the same kinds of suffering are being experienced by your brotherhood throughout the world." *(1 Peter 5:8-9)*.

"For by grace you have been saved through faith. And this is not your own doing; it is the gift of God," *(Ephesians 2:8)*.

"And whatever you ask in prayer, you will receive, if you have faith." *(Matthew 21:22)*.

"Is anyone among you sick? Let him call for the elders of the church, and let them pray over him, anointing him with oil in the name of the Lord. And the prayer of faith will save the one who is sick, and the Lord will raise him up. And if he has committed sins, he will be forgiven." *(James:5-14-15)*.

Helmet Of Salvation

Represents the hope and assurance of salvation provided by God, acting as a shield for the mind against the darkness of this world. It signifies the believer's secure identity and protection in Christ, ensuring they are on God's side in the spiritual battle.

"The Lord looked and was displeased that there was no justice. He saw that there was no one, he was appalled that there was no one to intervene, so his own arm achieved salvation for him, and his own righteousness sustained him. He put on righteousness as his breastplate, and the helmet of salvation on his head; he put on the garments of vengeance and wrapped himself in zeal as in a cloak." *(Isaiah 59:10-17).*

"But let us who are of the day be sober, and put on the armor of faith and love, and for helmet the hope of salvation." *(1 Thessalonians 5:8).*

Be prepared at all times. Read, Pray, and Memorize Scripture

Armor Of God Prayer

Dear God

Today I put on the full Armor of God to guard my life against attack.

I put on the Belt of Truth to protect against lies and deception.

I put on the Breastplate of Righteousness to protect our hearts from temptations I battle.

I put on the Gospel of Peace on our feet, so we are ready to take Your light, wherever You find me this day. I choose to walk in the peace and freedom of Your Spirit and not be overcome with fear and anxious thoughts.

I take up Your Shield of Faith that will extinguish all the darts and threats hurled our way by the enemy. I believe in Your power to protect us and choose to trust in You.

I put on the Helmet of Salvation, which covers our minds and thoughts, reminding me I am a child of God, forgiven, set free, and saved by the grace of Christ Jesus.

I take up the Sword of the Spirit, Your very Word, and the one offensive weapon given to me for battle, which has the power to demolish strongholds, alive, active, and is sharper than any two-edged sword.

I ask for your help in remembering always keep Your full Armor on every day, for you give me all that I need to stand firm in this world.

Forgive us God, for the time I have been unprepared, too busy to care, or trying to fight and wrestle in my own strength.

Thank you for I never fight alone, for you are constantly at work on my behalf - shielding, protecting, strengthening, exposing deeds of darkness, bringing to light what needs to be known, and covering me from the cruel attacks I face even when I am unaware. In the Power of Jesus Christ, Amen.

Check your Armor of God daily to make sure your Armor is securely on and ready for battle. Remember, this is a gift from God to protect and defend you from any harm.

Never Take Your Armor Off!

Spiritual Warfare Scriptures

The concept of "God reading the word" refers to the idea that God's Word, often understood as the Bible, is a living and active force, a source of divine truth and guidance, and a reflection of God's character and will.

"Submit yourselves to God. Resist the devil, and he will flee from you." *(James 4:7).*

"You are from God, little children, and have overcome them; because greater is He who is in you than he who is in the world." *(1 John 4:4).*

"For though we live in the world, we do not wage war as the world does. The weapons we fight with are not the weapons of the world. On the contrary, they have divine power to demolish strongholds. We demolish arguments and every pretension that sets itself up against the knowledge of God, and we take captive every thought to make it obedient to Christ."
(2 Corinthians 10:3-5).

"Be self-controlled and alert. Your enemy the devil prowls around like a roaring lion looking for someone to devour. Resist him, standing firm in the faith." *(1 Peter. 5:8-9).*

"No weapon that is formed against you will prosper; and every tongue that accuses you in judgment you will condemn. This is the heritage of the servants of the Lord, and their vindication is from Me," declares the Lord." *(Isaiah 54:17).*

Put on the full armor of God, so that you can take your stand against the devil's schemes. For our struggle is not against flesh and blood, but against the rulers, against the authorities, against the powers of this dark world and against the spiritual forces of evil in the heavenly realms. Therefore put on the full armor of God, so that when the day of evil comes, you may be able to stand your ground, and after you have done everything, to stand. Stand firm then, with the belt of truth buckled around your waist, with the breastplate of righteousness in place, and with your feet fitted with the readiness that comes from the gospel of peace. In addition to all this, take up the shield of faith, with which you can extinguish all the flaming arrows of the evil one. Take the helmet of salvation and the sword of the Spirit, which is the word of God." *(Ephesians 6:11-17)*.

"In all these things, we are more than conquerors through Him who loved us." *(Romans 8:37)*.

"But thanks be to God, who gives us the victory through our Lord Jesus Christ" *(1 Corinthians 15:57)*.

"Not by might nor by power, but by My Spirit,' says the Lord of hosts." *(Zechariah 4:6)*.

"But the Lord is faithful, and he will strengthen you and protect you from the evil one".
(2 Thessalonians 3:3).

"Behold, I have given you authority to tread on serpents and scorpions, and over all the power of the enemy, and nothing shall hurt you." *(Luke 10:19)*.

"The thief comes only to steal and kill and destroy. I came that they may have life and have it abundantly." *(John 10:10)*.

"Truly I tell you, whatever you bind on earth will be bound in heaven, and whatever you loose on earth will be loosed in heaven. Again, truly I tell you that if two of you on earth agree about anything they ask for, it will be done for them by my Father in heaven." *(Matthew 18:18-19)*.

"The Lord will cause your enemies who rise against you to be defeated before you. They shall come out against you one way and flee before you seven ways." *(Deuteronomy 28:7)*.

"I have told you these things, so that in me you may have peace. In this world you will have trouble. But take heart! I have overcome the world." *(John 16:33)*.

"No temptation has overtaken you except what is common to mankind. And God is faithful; he will not let you be tempted beyond what you can bear. But when you are tempted, he will also provide a way out so that you can endure it." *(1 Corinthians 10:13)*.

"And you will know the truth, and the truth will set you free." *(John 8:32).*

"Do not be overcome with evil, but overcome evil with good." *(Romans 12:21).*

"And they have conquered him by the blood of the Lamb and by the word of their testimony, for they loved not their lives even unto death." *(Revelation 12:11).*

"Fight the good fight of the faith. Take hold of the eternal life to which you were called when you made your good confession in the presence of many witnesses." *(1 Timothy 6:12).*

"On this rock I will build my church, and the gates of hell shall not prevail against it." *(Matthew 16:8).*

"...the reason the Son of God appeared was to destroy the devil's work." *(1 John 3:8).*

"But they who wait for the Lord shall renew their strength; they shall mount up with wings like eagles; they shall run and not be weary; they shall walk and not faint." *(Isaiah 40:31).*

"One of your men puts to flight a thousand, for the Lord your God is He who fights for you, just as He promised you." *(Joshua 23:10).*

"Do not fear them, for the Lord your God is the one fighting for you." *(Deuteronomy 3:22).*

"What then shall we say to these things? If God is for us, who is against us?" *(Romans 8:31).*

"Through You we will push back our adversaries, through Your name we will trample down those who rise up against us." *(Psalm 44:5).*

"Have I not commanded you? Be strong and courageous! Do not tremble or be dismayed, for the Lord your God is with you wherever you go." *(Joshua 1:9).*

"For You have girded me with strength for battle; You have subdued under me those who rose up against me." *(Psalm. 18:39).*

"He who dwells in the shelter of the Most High will rest in the shadow of the Almighty. I will say of the Lord, He is my refuge and my fortress, my God, in whom I trust. Surely, he will save you under his wings you will find refuge; his faithfulness will be your shield and rampart…" *(Psalms 91:1-4).*

"This is what the Lord says to you: 'Do not be afraid or discouraged because of this vast army. For the battle is not yours, but God's." *(2 Chronicles 20:15).*

The battle belongs to the Lord, and He has the final victory!

How Demons Work

Open Doors

Demons Gain Access To People's Lives

God sees the human body as a dwelling place. Scripture calls the body of the believer the temple of the Holy Spirit. *(1 Corinthians 6:19)*. But Satan and his demons also see the human body as a place to live. "When an unclean spirit goes out of a man, he goes through dry places, seeking rest, and finds none. Then he says, 'I will return to my house from which I came.' And when he comes, he finds it empty, swept, and put in order. Then he goes and takes with him seven other spirits more wicked than himself, and they enter and dwell there; and the last state of that man is worse than the first." *(Matthew 12:43-45)*. The demon in this passage refers to man as his house. Demons crave bodies to live in and to express their nature through. Without such a body, they are restless because they have no home. But a demon cannot simply enter into any person that they choose; there must be an open door in the house for it to have entrance. There are several things that can open doors for demonic access into your life. These examples of open doors give demons a place to enter and dwell in you.

Ongoing Sin

When you fail to confess and repent of sin, you come into agreement with Satan, and this gives him a right to an area of your life. Blatant rebellious sin or ongoing hidden sin can be a demonic entry point. Paul warns that if you do not properly deal with anger, it can give place to Satan. *(Ephesians 4:26-27)*. When you cannot gain freedom from a sinful habit, there is the possibility that a demon needs to be cast out for you to be free.

Traumatic Experiences

When you go through a traumatic experience, it is possible for a demon to gain access. Being sinned against or exploited can open a door. For example, being abused sexually, physically, or verbally can give demons entry into your life and cause you to be bound by that traumatic experience. You may feel only hate, pain, and agony. Some people even turn away from God. It seems unfair that a person can become demonized through another person's action, but Satan does not play fair. Various types of traumatic events and all types of abuse can open the door to demonic oppression.

Believing Demons

Satan is called the father of lies. His demons know no other language but lies. When you believe his lies, you move into agreement with him. As he steals souls from God, his goal is to steal, kill, and destroy in any way he can. When you believe a lie about God or about yourself, you open the way for a demon to reinforce that lie in your life.

Exposure To Unholy Things

Being exposed to unholy things can open the door to demons. Some examples are certain books, pornography, horror movies, dark music, occult items or idols, Eight Ball, Pokémon, Dungeons and Dragons, Fortune Telling, Astrology, Witchcraft, Satanism, organizations or clubs that demands oaths and vows, any representation of the Devil, demons, pagan gods or goddesses in jewelry, art, books, non-Biblical Religions Yoga, Hinduism, Ancient Religions practices, including art, books, music, and jewelry. There are many more. There is a reason why God commands His people to come out from among the world and be holy.

Unforgiveness

Having unforgiveness in your life gives permission for demons to influence you. Do not neglect unforgiveness in your life - yourself as well as others. To be set free, you must forgive anyone who has hurt you. To be set free, you must also forgive yourself for any sins you have committed.

Having bitterness, resentment, or unforgiveness toward others is an open door for demons. The parable of the unmerciful servant shows how the unforgiving servant is put into prison to be tormented. *(Matthew 18:21-35)*. Withholding forgiveness from others puts you into a spiritual prison and gives the devil permission to torment you. This is a serious issue and a major root cause for many other problems. You must learn to choose to forgive the ones who have hurt you. This is done through the same grace that Christ gave to all of us through His Crucifixion and Resurrection. This does not mean that something bad someone did to you is okay. It does not mean you should not maintain boundaries with those who hurt you. It does mean you are called to walk in forgiveness. This is the same forgiveness God gave you through the Cross and the Resurrection of Jesus Christ.

Involvement in False Religion, Cults, and False Teaching

Behind every idol is a demon *(1 Corinthians 10:19-20)*, and false teaching carries with it a false spirit *(2 Corinthians 11:4),* and *(1 Timothy 4:1)*. It makes sense that those who become involved with cults and who believe false teachings can become targets of demons. If it is an obviously false teaching like Buddhism, Hinduism, the worship of idols, gods, Satan, or even using subtle erroneous teachings within the church can open a door for demons to enter.

"Father, forgive me for partnering with any false teaching, cults, and idols. I repent for any participation and ask for your forgiveness. Amen"

Any Occult Involvement

Contact with the occult is definitely an open door to the demonic and is strictly forbidden in Scripture *(Deuteronomy 18:9-12)*. There are two sources of supernatural power in the world: God and Satan. The word occult means "secret or hidden" and refers to the supernatural realm of Satan. Some examples include Witchcraft, fortunetelling, communication with the dead, magic arts, eastern meditation, sorcery, Ouija board, astrology, Satanism, new age teachings, psychics, astral projection, and channeling. This is not an all-inclusive list, but should give you an idea of what to avoid. If you have had any contact with the occult, even if it was a long time ago, and it was just for fun. Renounce your involvement by praying out loud.

"Father I repent, renounce, and ask for you forgiveness for any involvement I have had with _____ Amen"

To be sure all curses or demonic activities are broken, seek out Deliverance Ministry.

Demonic Footholds

Spiritual Footholds are situations, circumstances, or patterns of behavior that provide an opportunity for demonic influence to enter your life. "Satanic footholds" are a secure, strategic position from which demons can advance. These footholds are areas where Satan can enter and exert his influence. Satan and his demons gain influence over you through various demonic actions and attitudes. These actions and attitudes create opportunities for him to exert his power. It is like being pulled down into the unknown depths of despair and doubt. In his distress, the psalmist cried out to God for salvation. "I sink in the murky depths, where there is no foothold. I have come into the deep waters; the floods engulf me." *(Psalm 69:2).*

As a Christian, Satan is looking to establish a strategic position in your life. It may be through something as simple as holding on to anger, grudges, and bitterness. Once Satan establishes a foothold, He is always finding ways to make further advances into your life. He will continue to spread his lies and multiple temptations. Eventually, his foothold will become a Stronghold. If you give Satan a foothold in your life, he will have an easier time attacking you, as he works on separating you from God. The more and the stronger footholds will eventually become a Spiritual Stronghold. Spiritual Strongholds are habitual thought patterns or mental fortresses that can prevent you from growing in your faith and living according to God's will. "And do not give the devil a foothold." *(Ephesians 4:27).*

Addressing satanic footholds is seen as a part of spiritual warfare. It is a process of resisting the influence of evil forces and seeking God's protection and strength. Understanding the concept of demonic footholds and choosing to prevent and to remove any footholds allows you to turn from guilt and shame. This is the end of these footholds in your life. Paul says the best way to deal with these negative emotions is immediately. This stands true for all negative emotions. "Do not let the sun go down while you are still angry, for anger gives a foothold to the devil." *(Ephesians 4:26b-27).*

How Do We Go About Giving Demons A Foothold?

Should you engage in certain negative behaviors, thoughts, attitudes, or sins, you can inadvertently provide demons opportunities to gain footholds in your life. Unresolved issues or persistent sins can create vulnerabilities that demons can exploit. As a Christian, this allows demons to influence your mind, body, and emotions. As a non-Christian, they are able to influence your mind, body, emotions, and soul.

Footholds Entry Points

Footholds' entry points can include negative actions like unforgiveness, anger, resentment, bitterness, gossip, lust, pride, persistent sin, and lack of faith in God. Negative emotions and behaviors can give Demons a point of entry. There are situations, circumstances, or patterns of behavior that provide opportunities for demonic influence to enter your life.

The Impact Of Footholds

By allowing these things to take root, you open yourself up to further influence and spiritual harm from Satan. Once a foothold is established, demons will seek to worsen the situation, leading to more severe spiritual problems like mental and emotional distress, addictions, or even physical ailments.

Breaking Footholds

Recognizing and addressing footholds through prayer, repentance, confession of sins, seeking God's guidance, and Deliverance can help break these demonic footholds. When you break these footholds, you can reclaim spiritual freedom in your life.

Demonic Strongholds

The word strongholds is found once in the New Testament. It is used symbolically by Paul in a description of the Christian's spiritual battle: "For though we live in the world, we do not wage war as the world does. The weapons we fight with are not the weapons of the world. On the contrary, they have divine power to demolish strongholds. We demolish arguments and every pretension that sets itself up against the knowledge of God, and we take captive every thought to make it obedient to Christ. Though we walk in the flesh, we do not war according to the flesh, for the weapons of our warfare are not of the flesh, but divinely powerful for the destruction of fortresses [strongholds]" *(2 Corinthians 10:3-5).*

Spiritual strongholds are habitual thought patterns or mental fortresses that can prevent you from growing in your faith and living according to God's will. These strongholds are often rooted in lies or negative beliefs that have become deeply ingrained, making it difficult to break free from them. They can manifest as limiting perceptions, negative emotions, dysfunctional behaviors, or a resistance to change. Spiritual Strongholds of believers are like fortified areas of the emotions, the mind, and the body. Spiritual Strongholds of Non-Believers include the mind, emotions, body, and soul. Strongholds actively resist God's truth and hinder spiritual growth.

They are often described as harmful thought patterns or beliefs that hinder your growth and relationship with God. Spiritual strongholds are persistent, often subconscious thought patterns or beliefs that hinder spiritual growth. They can lead to harmful behaviors. Strongholds are mental, spiritual barriers that hinder spiritual growth and prevent individuals from living according to God's will. Recognizing and breaking these strongholds through truth, prayer, and spiritual warfare is essential for experiencing true freedom and an abundant life.

Strongholds are not demons themselves, but demonic forces can operate within them. Strongholds developed by demonic interference influence habitual ways of thinking and behaving that create mental and emotional barriers to God's work in your life. Even though Strongholds are not demons themselves, demons can operate within them. This led to negative behaviors and outcomes. Strongholds are places where ungodly influences can take root and thrive. Demons can keep you from thinking clearly, accepting the truth, repeating of sin, and receiving Deliverance. Some Strongholds are confusion, fear, anger, and unforgiveness. They manifest in many other forms.

Strongholds can develop with repeated exposure to negative thoughts, unbiblical false beliefs, harmful behavior, negative childhood experiences, societal pressure, and personal choices. Also, disobeying God's Word, disregarding His counsel, and dwelling on self-worship. Recognizing strongholds often involves identifying recurring patterns of thought or behavior that are difficult to change, even when they contradict God's truth.

Overcoming Strongholds requires a committed effort to identify and dismantle all of the negative patterns of your thinking and behavior. It can be helped through Deliverance, and it can be achieved through prayer, study of God's Word, seeking guidance from trusted spiritual mentors, and practicing forgiveness and humility. Breaking off Strongholds involves replacing the lies and false beliefs with God's truth, and negative habits with healthy choices.

Demonic Soul Ties

A soul tie is expressed through a feeling of a profound sense of connection with someone. Soul Ties can be positive, building healthy bonds with others. But they can also be negative, which hinders spiritual growth and creates unhealthy dependencies. Ungodly soul ties are those that are built on sin, such as codependency, unhealthy attachments, lack of boundaries, and sex without marriage. All soul ties a lack of boundaries.

Demonic Soul Ties can bring in negative emotional, spiritual, or even physical harm. While the term "soul tie" is not explicitly used in the Bible, the concept is clearly present. Demonic soul ties are formed when two individuals share a strong negative emotional or spiritual connection. They can form through various interactions, including romantic relationships, close friendships, prolonged interactions at work, family connections, vows and agreements, trauma and abuse, and spiritual practices.

Breaking Demonic Soul ties refers to the process of breaking unhealthy emotional and spiritual bonds with others. Particularly those that are based on ungodly principles or relationships. To break negative connections, you need to identify, confess, and repent through Jesus Christ. It is important to break all negative or sinful Soul Ties to achieve total freedom.

Demonic Soul ties can be formed through:

Unhealthy Emotional Dependence:

Feeling anxious when separated from the other person, needing their approval or validation, or having difficulty making decisions without their input.

Inability to Move Forward:

Feeling stuck in a past relationship or pattern, unable to move on or find new connections.

Jealousy or Possessiveness:

Experiencing intense feelings of jealousy or possessiveness towards the other person, or difficulty trusting them.

Feeling of Being Controlled:

Feeling that the other person is controlling or manipulating your thoughts, emotions, or behavior.

Intense Spiritual Connection:

Feeling our souls are united as one, and that the "tie" is binding you to a person you do not want to be bound to, and is hampering your efforts at moving forward in life.

Persistent Feelings of Shame and Unworthiness:

Feeling depressed, shame, feeling you are not good enough, or unworthy of affection.

Sinful Actions:

Engaging in actions that are harmful to yourself or others, such as infidelity, addiction, or abuse.

Unexplained Emotional Turmoil:

Feeling an emotional connection that causes pain or suffering.

Repent of Sexual Relationships Outside of Marriage.

Sexual relationships outside of marriage can produce demonic Soul Ties. Each Soul Tie can be an entry point for demons. These ties must be broken by confessing them as sin, asking for forgiveness, and choosing to be free from them.

"Father, I confess the sin of sexual relations outside of marriage. I renounce that sinful activity in Jesus's name and ask for Your forgiveness." Amen

When you unite yourself with a person out of wedlock, you become as one body, and you open the door to demonic intrusion. For it is said, 'The two will become one flesh.' But whoever is united with the Lord is one with him in spirit." *(1 Corinthians 6:16-17)*. This highlights the spiritual impact of sexual unions and the importance of being united with the Lord, instead of ungodly connections. Christ has "canceled the charge of our legal indebtedness, which stood against us and condemned us; He has taken it away, nailing it to the cross." *(Colossians 2:14)*.

It is through Christ, you have the power to be free from spiritual bondages, including Soul Ties, by doing the following.

Acknowledge the Need:

Begin by honestly acknowledging the need for breaking the Soul Tie and the hurt it has caused.

Seek Repentance, Forgiveness, and Healing:

Repent of anything you did to participate in the Soul Tie. Ask God for forgiveness for any part you played in the relationship and for healing from any emotional wounds.

Renounce Unhealthy Agreements:

Explicitly renounce any vows, agreements, or commitments that are not in line with God's will.

Request for the Soul Tie to Be Broken:

Ask God to break any unholy bonds and sever any connections that are not pleasing to Him.

Surrender to God:

Express your desire to surrender your heart and life to God's guidance and love.

Pray in Faith:

Pray with faith, believing that God is able to break the soul tie and restore you to wholeness.

Personalize Your Prayer:

Tailor the prayer to your specific situation and needs, using your own words and expressing your heart to God.

Breaking Soul Ties Through Prayer

"Lord, I ask for your guidance and strength, so that all unhealthy Soul Ties can be broken. I acknowledge that I have been hurt, and I repent that I have hurt others. I ask for your forgiveness and healing. I renounce any unholy agreements or vows that I may have made, and I ask that you sever any connections that are not pleasing to You. Amen"

For each person you can think of, say out loud with their name inserted in the blank. Keep going until you cannot remember anyone else. If you cannot remember their name, say "that person". If you remember someone later, pause and repeat the phrase below.

In the name of Jesus Christ, I break every soul tie and every unholy bond with _____.

I give back what I took from_____ and I take back what I gave _____.

"I surrender my heart to you Lord, and I ask that you fill me with your love and peace. In Your Holy name, Amen".

Generational Curses

Negative patterns of behavior or sin can be passed down through generations, creating generational footholds that need to be addressed. "The Lord will by no means clear the guilty, but will visit the iniquity of the fathers on the children and on the grandchildren, to the third and fourth generation." *(Exodus 34:7)*.

At the moment of conversion, Christians are enlisted in a spiritual army and are involved in a spiritual war. They immediately become an enemy of Satan. "Finally, be strong in the Lord and in his mighty power. Put on the full armor of God, so that you can take your stand against the devil's schemes. For our struggle is not against flesh and blood, but against the rulers, against the authorities, against the powers of this dark world and against the spiritual forces of evil in the heavenly realms." *(Ephesians 6:10–12)*. Paul warns you against giving the devil a foothold: "In your anger do not sin. Do not let the sun go down while you are still angry, and do not give the devil a foothold." *(Ephesians 4:26–27)*.

Generational Curses can produce misfortune, negative traits, and negative behaviors, especially dysfunctional behaviors. They are often rooted in sin or trauma. Generational Cures are passed from generation to generation. The experiences of our ancestors can create a negative legacy and impact subsequent generations.

Until the Generational Curses are broken, they can lead to future family members repeating the sins and negative patterns of their ancestors. "You shall not bow down to them nor serve them. For I, the Lord your God, am a jealous God, visiting the iniquity of the fathers upon the children to the third and fourth generations of those who hate Me, but showing mercy to thousands, to those who love Me and keep My commandments." *(Exodus 20:5-6)*. "The Lord is slow to anger and abounding in steadfast love, forgiving iniquity and to the third and the fourth generation." *(Hebrews 14:18)*.

Breaking Generational Curses

When you break generational curses, you are making the conscious decision to stop practicing, absorbing, and passing on toxic behaviors and personality traits to your children and your future generations. Some of these toxic personality traits can be anger, violence, manipulation, lying, being overly critical, cheating, stealing, and addiction, just to name a few. The sins of your ancestors can and are being passed from generation to generation. This is particularly true of addictive behaviors, such as alcoholism, drugs, sex, but can also include lying, depression, anger, stealing, and murder, plus many more. Similarly, receiving physical and sexual abuse can become embedded in the legacy of certain families. Deliverance from these curses is available to everyone who sincerely wants to be healed from the trauma and calls upon the name of Jesus. "Therefore there is now no condemnation for those who in Christ Jesus." *(Romans 8:1).* "... everyone who calls on the name of the Lord will be saved." *(Romans 10:13).*

Jesus does challenge the concept of inherited guilt by offering individual redemption, which frees believers from condemnation and replaces it with God's grace and righteousness. Instead of being held responsible for the sins of others, Christians can receive a "new creation" in Christ, where past sin and guilt are done away with and replaced by God's love and acceptance. When Jesus' disciples asked if a blind man was born blind because of his own sins or his parents' sins, Jesus responds, "Neither this man nor his parents sinned, but this happened so that the works of God might be displayed in his life." *(John 9:2-3).* This gospel is based on receiving this gift of justification through faith, not through earning it by means of good works or being punished for a guilt that was not your own. "And do not be conformed to this world, but be transformed by the renewal of your mind, that by testing you may discern what is the will of God, what is acceptable and perfect." *(Romans 12:1-2).*

It is important that you have this kind of faith and exhibit it boldly, so that you can accept this gift from God. Unfortunately, in some cases, there are people who need help to overcome the sins of their ancestors (Generational Curses). The sins of their families have been displayed for generations, and individual family members have never recovered.

Spiritual and Religious Interpretations

Biblical concept:

In some religious contexts, the term is tied to the biblical idea that the consequences of sin can affect descendants for a certain number of generations, often linked to concepts like "iniquity".

Spiritual beliefs:

Some spiritual beliefs include the idea that negative spiritual influences or rituals from ancestors can have ongoing effects on their descendants.

Breaking the cycle:

Many spiritual perspectives emphasize faith, repentance, and God's grace as ways to break these cycles. This suggests that these are not insurmountable forces.

Engage in spiritual practices through Deliverance

For those who follow a spiritual path, engaging in prayer, repentance, or other faith-based practices may be a component of breaking the cycle

Acknowledge the patterns:

Recognize and identify the recurring negative behaviors or situations within your family history.

Change learned behaviors:

Consciously work to change unhealthy patterns by modeling different behaviors for yourself and any future generations.

Address trauma:

Process and heal from past or ancestral traumas through therapy or other healing practices.

How to Break Generational Curses

While the Bible acknowledges the impact of past sins, it also emphasizes the importance of repentance, forgiveness, and seeking God's grace to overcome generational patterns of sin. If you are living under a generational curse, it will be canceled when you, through faith, repent and renounce the curse.

A Prayer to Repent and Break Off Generational Curses

Fill in the blank below with the name of one person in your family. This person you identify as exhibiting ongoing sin. Repeat until you cannot remember any more names. If you should remember another name later, stop repent for the sins of that person. Should you not be able to remember a specific name, just say that person.

Father,

I repent of my sins and those of _____(name of ancestor)

I break every oath, every vow, pledge, and ceremony. I renounce it all now and put it under the blood of Jesus.

Pray this Prayer upon completion.

"I thank you, God, that generational curses are broken through faith in the Lord Jesus. I believe Jesus is my strength and that His blood cancels any curse and breaks any generational sins. I believe that any generational curse is canceled and broken off my family now, in Jesus' name. Thank you that sins, bondages, and iniquities are canceled and any curse is stopped by the blood of Jesus. Thank you that through Jesus, no curse will be passed to another generation. Amen."

Spiritual Trauma

Spiritual trauma refers to the impact of traumatic events on your sense of meaning, self-concept, and your relationship with and faith in God. In some cases, it can involve questioning your faith or feeling abandoned by God. Spiritual abuse is demonic and a form of emotional manipulation. The trauma is made worse by using religious beliefs or authority structures to justify abusive behavior. A traumatic event can cause you to experience changes in the way you see God, such as feeling abandoned or punished by Him, feeling angry at Him, or questioning how the loving, all-powerful God could allow horrible things to happen to the innocent. All of which are demonic thoughts that can lead you into questioning God.

Your spiritual life is helpful in building a closer relationship with God. This close relationship to God buffers the effects of a traumatic event and gives you a source of comfort during times of distress. After a traumatic event, a close relationship with God can happen because you have the opportunity to increase your faith in Him. Your relationship with God can become even more meaningful to you. When this happens, you find a greater sense of purpose in your life and a new closeness to God. You experience the ability to work with God to solve problems, relieve pain, and give forgiveness.

To achieve all of this freedom, God gave you the ability to forgive yourself and others, just as He forgave you. Jesus emphasizes the importance of forgiveness from God, as well as your forgiveness of others. His teachings highlight forgiveness as a core principle for believers. Urging you to forgive others as you have been forgiven by God. Forgiveness is a key to our relationship with others and with Him. This is shown clearly in the Lord's Prayer, where Jesus teaches, "Forgive us our debts, as we also have forgiven our debtors" *(Matthew 6:12).*

A traumatic event can cause you to experience changes in the way you see God, such as feelings of being abandoned or punished by Him, feeling angry at Him because He did not step in and stop the abuse, or questioning how a loving, all-powerful God can allow horrible things to happen to the innocent. When you struggle to make sense of a trauma, your belief in God may falter, and unforgiveness then takes hold. All of this opens a door for demons to step right in. Demons can cause you to feel there is no God, God does not care, God does not love you, God is punishing you, and if God really cared, this would have never happened.

Where was Jesus? With the experience of this type of traumatic event, you can think that this is punishment from God. You feel that the world is more cruel than you thought. God really is not that good, Jesus really does not care, and the Holy Spirit does not exist. This causes more spiritual injury and guilt, and as forgiving others can become impossible. Demons rejoice because there is a victim they can control and influence. They will entice you to see life as negative or evil. But, more importantly to demons, you believe there is no God. Without your repentance and turning back to God, they just stole a soul from God.

All of this opens doors for demons to influence or control your life. Not only your personal spiritual life, but also your relationship with God. There is less or perhaps no forgiveness given. There is less relationship with God, and there is less prayer life. There is less reading of the Bible for direction. There is definitely less reliance on God for anything. And, the worst for you is to think there is no God and you decide to walk away from Him. This trauma can also lead to mental illness or suicide. So, things can get much worse due to trauma. All demons that take over the mind, body, and emotions are delighted.

What To Do?

For peace of mind, it is important for you to face into the trauma, as God holds you up. He is good and has already defeated Satan and all of demons. There is hope for now as well as in the future. God loves you more than you can imagine. He is listening to you, cares for you, and guides you. God is good. He protects you and holds you in the palm of His hand. He is there with you always, even in the worst of times. Even though it does not seem God is there at all, God holds you up, comforts, and protects you no matter the circumstances.

Psalm 91 is a powerful declaration of faith and trust in God's protection and provision. It emphasizes God's love and care for those who love Him, offering assurances of security and deliverance in times of trouble. The psalmist speaks of God as a refuge and a fortress, promising to shield and protect those who dwell in His presence. It is important to trust God's power, the power that created the Universe. We need to trust in that same power and seek His presence.

His outstretched arms are waiting for you to take refuge from Him and to trust in His ability to protect and guide you. He is constantly involved in you and your life. He cares and brings comfort to you in times of need, even if you do not recognize it immediately. He never turns away from you. God provides you strength and comfort even when you face terrible hardships. He never leaves you, even if you do not feel His presence. He is always there with hope and assurance, and you are never alone. In the worst of times, all you have to do is turn your face towards Him. Know that He is the God of love, compassion, understanding, patience, and has the strength to carry you when you need Him to.

"Whoever dwells in the shelter of the Most High will rest in the shadow of the Almighty I will say of the Lord, 'He is my refuge and my fortress, my God, in whom I trust.'"

"Surely he will save you from the fowler's snare and from the deadly pestilence. He will cover you with his feathers, and under his wings you will find refuge; his faithfulness will be your shield and rampart. You will not fear the terror of night, nor the arrow that flies by day, nor the pestilence that stalks in the darkness, nor the plague that destroys at midday. A thousand may fall at your side, ten thousand at your right hand, but it will not come near you. You will only observe with your eyes and see the punishment of the wicked. If you say, "The Lord is my refuge," and you make the Most High your dwelling, no harm will overtake you, no disaster will come near your tent. For he will command his angels concerning you to guard you in all your ways; they will lift you up in their hands, so that you will not strike your foot against a stone. You will tread on the lion and the cobra; you will trample the great lion and the serpent.

"Because he loves me," says the Lord, "I will rescue him; I will protect him, for he acknowledges my name. He will call on me, and I will answer him; I will be with him in trouble, I will deliver him and honor him. With long life I will satisfy him and show him my salvation." *(Psalm 91).*

Satanism

It is a group of religious, ideological, or philosophical beliefs based on Satan, particularly his worship and adoration. Satanism's religious, ideological, and philosophical beliefs counter the beliefs of the Jewish, Christian, and Islamic religions.

In Judaism, Satan is seen as an agent subservient to God, typically regarded as a symbol for evil. In Christianity and Islam, he is usually seen as a fallen angel or jinn, a supernatural being from pre-Islamic Arabian and Islamic tradition.

Satan has rebelled against God, who nevertheless allows him temporary power over the fallen world and a host of demons. Satan shares historical connections and resemblances to other occult figures like:
Asmodeus, Beelzebub, Hecate, Lilith, Lucifer, Mephistopheles, Pan , and Prometheus.

Historical context

Accusations of groups engaged in "devil worship" have echoed throughout much of Christian history. During the Middle Ages, the Inquisition led by the Catholic Church alleged that various heretical Christian sects and groups, such as the Knights Templar and the Cathars, are movements that believed there is a God of heaven and an evil one, Satan, the master of the physical world. The Knights Templar and the Cathars both performed secret Satanic rituals.

In the Early Modern period, belief in a widespread Satanic conspiracy of witches resulted in the trials and executions of tens of thousands of alleged witches across Europe and the North American colonies. The deaths peaked between 1560 and 1630.

While accusations of devil worship have been used to persecute various groups for centuries, modern, organized theistic Satanism is a more recent phenomenon, with many groups forming after the rise of atheistic Satanism in the 1960s.

The terms Satanist and Satanism emerged in the church during the Reformation and Counter-Reformation (1517–1700). Since the 19th century, various small religious groups have identified themselves as Satanists or used Satanic images and symbols. While the groups that appeared after the 1960s differed greatly, they can be broadly divided into atheistic Satanism and theistic Satanism. Those worshiping Satan as a supernatural deity relate to Satan as a patriarch. Nonreligious Satanists regard Satan as a symbol of certain human traits. Contemporary religious Satanism is predominantly an American phenomenon, although the rise of globalization and the Internet has seen these ideas spread to other parts of the world.

A person self-identifying as a member of Satanism is a relatively modern phenomenon, largely attributed to the 1966 founding of the Church of Satan in the United States. This group does not believe in a supernatural Satan, but as a symbol aligned with atheistic and non-theistic philosophy.

Modern Day Satanism

Rituals and Practices

There are broad and modern counter-cultural religions with diverse interpretations, most of which do not involve the worship of an evil deity. The beliefs, philosophies, and practices of Satanic groups vary significantly, but they generally use Satan as a symbol of rebellion against arbitrary authority, individualism, and free will. However, there are Satanists today who do worship Lucifer, cast spells, and hold satanic rituals.

Actual Worship:

Unlike atheistic Satanists, Theistic followers may perform rituals and prayers with the intent of communicating with or worshiping Satan as a divine force.

Black magic and occultism:

Theistic Satanism is more commonly associated with various types of magic and occult practices, and may involve borrowing from other esoteric traditions.

Theistic Satanism:

In contrast to atheistic forms, some Satanists genuinely believe in Satan as a supernatural deity whom they revere or worship. However, they do not necessarily view Satan as omnipotent or evil in the Christian sense, often relating to him as a patriarch or source of enlightenment. Some of these practitioners may view their beliefs as separate from Christian interpretations entirely.

Reverence for a divine being:

They believe in Satan as a real entity to be revered or petitioned to. However, their view of Satan is often different from the Christian concept of an evil force. Instead, Satan may be seen as a source of freedom, knowledge, and personal empowerment.

Diverse Traditions:

Beliefs are highly individualistic and vary widely. Some groups incorporate practices and deities from pre-Christian religions, Gnosticism, or other occult traditions.

Spiritual growth:

This path is often focused on the practitioner's self-deification or individual spiritual evolution, with Satan acting as a guide or mentor.

Worship of Lucifer:

Some groups identify as Luciferians rather than Satanists, viewing Lucifer as a bringer of enlightenment and knowledge rather than as an evil figure. They often distinguish themselves from both atheistic and other theistic forms of Satanism. Satanist rituals vary dramatically depending on the specific type of Satanism, which can be either atheistic or theistic.

Atheistic Satanism:

Followers do not believe in supernatural beings, including God and Satan. The Church of Satan philosophy views Satan as a symbol of individualism, rebellion, self-empowerment, and carnal existence. They reject the Jewish, Christian, and Islamic beliefs. They embrace concepts like indulgence, undefiled wisdom, and personal responsibility

They do not involve supernatural worship and instead use rituals as a form of psychological self-empowerment or political protest. The two most prominent atheistic Satanist organizations are the Church of Satan, founded by Anton LaVey in 1966, and The Satanic Temple, founded by Lucien Greaves and Malcolm Jarry in 2013. Their rituals reflect their distinct philosophies.

The Church of Satan

Views ritual as a psychodrama for emotional and psychological liberation, rather than worship.

- **Greater Magic:** This category of ritual is used for self-transformation and is detailed in *The Satanic Bible*. The three main types are:
- **Lust Rituals:** Designed to attract a desired romantic or sexual partner.
- **Compassion Rituals:** Aimed at gaining success, improving health, or assisting those the Satanist cares about.

- **Destruction Rituals:** Intended to purge a member's anger toward an enemy by ritually destroying them.
- **Lesser Magic:** This involves psychological manipulation and "wile and guile" to influence others and situations to one's will.
- **Black Mass:** Their own version of a Black Mass is an act of deconditioning. It is a theatrical parody of the Roman Catholic Mass used to free the participant from inhibitions developed under Christian society.

The Satanic Temple

This is a prominent atheistic and politically active organization that uses the Satanic figure as a symbol of rebellion against tyrannical authority. It focuses on secular activism and challenging the influence of religion in public life, with beliefs that emphasize compassion, reason, and justice. It uses Satanic imagery for social and political activism, with rituals often symbolizing personal liberation. It is distinct from the Church of Satan and often opposes its more individualistic beliefs.

Rituals

- **Unbaptism:** A symbolic rite in which participants reject superstitions and renounce a religious ceremony (such as a Christian baptism) that was imposed on them without their consent as a child.
- **Destruction Ritual:** A member destroys an object that symbolizes a source of pain in their life.
- **Religious Abortion Ritual:** This ritual is part of their campaign to protect reproductive rights. It exempts members from legally mandated, non-medical procedures, like waiting periods, based on religious freedom. The ritual involves reciting TST tenets and a personal affirmation.
- **Black Mass:** They also hold Black Masses as celebrations of blasphemy to express personal liberty and freedom.

- **Atheistic Satanism:** Atheistic Satanists, unlike their atheistic counterparts, believe in Satan as a real, spiritual being and often engage in devotional practices.
- **Worship and Invocation:** Practices may include prayer, offerings, and invocation rituals aimed at forming a spiritual connection with Satan or other demonic entities. The nature of this deity varies, but it is often seen as a bringer of freedom, knowledge, and self-empowerment, rather than an evil figure.
- **Magic:** Theistic Satanists may perform magic to achieve goals by working with spiritual entities.
- **Individualistic Practice:** Theistic Satanism does not have a single, unified doctrine. Rituals are highly individualistic and can be influenced by other esoteric traditions.

Witchcraft

Witches in Society

Historical and anthropological human research suggests that nearly all societies have developed the idea of a sinister and anti-human force that can hide itself within society. This includes a belief in witches, a group of individuals who oppose the norms of their society and seek to harm their community by engaging in incest, murder, and cannibalism. Allegations of witchcraft may have different causes and serve different functions within a society. For instance, they may serve to uphold their social norms, to heighten the tension in existing conflicts between individuals, or to blame certain individuals for various social problems.

Another contributing factor about witches is the concept that there is an agent of misfortune and evil who operates on a cosmic scale. They believe in a strong form of opposition that divides the world clearly into forces of good and forces of evil.

At the very beginning, the earliest evil was the snake that appeared in this world in the Garden of Eden. This concept of evil was embraced by Judaism and early Christianity. It was soon marginalized within Jewish thought, but gained increasing importance within early Christian's understanding of how good and evil work in the world. They began to believe that God, in His mercy, provided us our salvation, forgives us of our sins, and lives within us.

Modern witches are individuals of diverse beliefs. Their practice is spirituality rooted in nature and self-empowerment. They practice spiritual rituals, some of which are performed during the Earth's equinoxes. They are a growing community, influenced by rituals and traditions practiced outside the main world religions, especially those of pre-Christian Europe and North America. They have a desire to reclaim feminine power, often engaging in activities like environmentalism, personal healing, and divination. Many witches practice outside of formal structures and personalize their own path. This is a prominent witchcraft tradition today.

Witch curses can refer to historical beliefs about harm caused by witches, symbolic or ritualistic magic intended to cause misfortune, or, in modern practice, a type of spell that some witches use to cause harm. Historically, curses were believed to cause ailments, bad luck, or death, and were associated with practices like using tag locks (items belonging to the victim) or symbolic objects like voodoo dolls. Some modern witches reject cursing due to ethical beliefs, while others view it as a tool for justice or self-expression when other methods fail.

Wicca is a specific religion. It is common for Wiccans to practice duo-theistic worship of a Horned God and a Mother Goddess. While witches are practitioners of witchcraft, Wicca practitioners, Wiccans, follow a modern, Earth-centered religion that honors nature through ritual and magic. The practitioners of Wicca typically believe that they were the deities that were worshipped by the hunter-gatherers who lived during the Stone Age.

Many Wiccans believe in magic, a manipulative force used through the practice of "Spell-Craft". Wicca generally prohibits curses. The Wiccan Rede, a central ethical code, teaches followers to "And ye harm none, do what ye will," meaning that Wiccans should avoid causing harm to others. Cursing, which intentionally inflicts harm, directly violates this principle.

Curses

In the West, we tend to think that the idea of curses is a superstitious belief, but it is found in the Bible over 200 times. A curse is used to invoke a supernatural power, to inflict harm or punishment on someone or something. It is often delivered through spoken or written words. It can also refer to a profane or obscene expression of anger, or to the misfortune that results from such a wish. In religious contexts, a curse is often seen as a judgment or a withdrawal of divine favor.

Definitions of a Curse

A Wish for harm

A verbal or written invocation intended to bring evil or harm upon a person, place, or object.

Profane language

A word or expression used in anger, frustration, or disgust, such as an oath or obscenity.

Misfortune

An evil or misfortune that occurs as if in response to a curse.

Malicious curses

These are cast with the specific intention of harming a target due to hatred, anger, or jealousy. The negative effects can range from bad luck and misfortune to physical ailment or death.

Protective curses

These are intended to guard a person, place, or object. They act as a deterrent, with the punishment automatically activating against anyone who disrespects a sacred boundary or tries to steal a protected item.

Self-curses

In some traditions, a person might bring a curse upon themselves through their own actions or desires. The consequences often serve as a form of karmic retribution.

Generational curses

These are afflictions passed down through a family line, where the sins of one generation cause problems for those who follow. In some interpretations, this curse can be broken through repentance and faith.

Another type of curse is what is called a word curse, "but no human being can tame the tongue. It is a restless evil, full of deadly poison. With the tongue we praise our Lord and Father, and with it we curse human beings, who have been made in God's likeness. Out of the same mouth come praise and cursing. My brothers and sisters, this should not be." *(James 3:8-10).*

"The tongue has the power of life and death, and those who love it will eat its fruit". *(Proverbs 18:21).*

Personal Sin

Personal sin refers to individual actions, words, or desires that are considered an offense against a divine law, an action of free will that is contrary to God's will. "So whoever knows the right thing to do and fails to do it, for him it is sin." *(James 4:17)*.

Types of personal sins:

The Seven Deadly Sins:

A traditional classification includes pride, greed, wrath, envy, gluttony, lust, and sloth.

Actions:

Specific acts like lying, stealing, murder, adultery, blasphemy, and idolatry.

Internal acts:

Sinful desires, words, or thoughts, such as anger, envy, or lust.

Sins of Omission:

Failing to do something one should, such as not helping the poor or not disclosing a sin when one is obligated to.

Christian classifications

Mortal Sin:

Grave offenses committed with full knowledge and deliberate consent. They are seen as a rejection of God, destroying charity, and, if unreconciled, can lead to eternal separation from God.

Venial Sin:

Sins that are less severe and do not cut the person off from God's grace, but still harm the relationship with God.

Due to personal sin, it is important that you maintain spiritual growth, healing, and a healthy relationship with God. It involves acknowledging wrongdoing, feeling regret, and committing to a change. This allows you to seek forgiveness from God for your sinful actions, thoughts, and deeds. Through God's Grace, you can move forward with a renewed sense of purpose and peace.

A prayer for Forgiveness.

"Dear God, thank You for Your promise to forgive me when I confess my sins. I confess my [specific known sins] and ask for Your mercy. Forgive me for my sin and create in me a clean heart. I receive Your forgiveness and trust in Your grace to guide me, Amen."

Occult

The occult refers to a category of beliefs and practices that are considered hidden or secret, often involving supernatural, mystical, or magical phenomena that fall outside the scope of mainstream science and organized religion. It comes from the Latin word occultus, meaning "hidden" or "concealed," and includes a wide range of traditions and practices, such as alchemy, astrology, divination, and witchcraft.

Occult practices and belief:

Magic

Practices that aim to manipulate reality through supernatural means. Magic refers to the belief and practice of influencing supernatural forces. It includes practices like divination and alchemy.

Astrology

The belief that the positions and movements of celestial bodies influence human affairs and can be used for divination.

Alchemy

A practice that combined scientific and philosophical traditions, believing in a connection between matter, mind, religion, and astrology. A historical tradition involving the transformation of matter, often with symbolic and spiritual interpretations.

Divination:

The practice of seeking hidden knowledge of the future through supernatural means such as omens, tarot cards, palmistry, crystal balls, or Ouija boards. often used to gain insight into situations, solve problems, or provide spiritual guidance. Divination can be categorized into inductive (reading signs), interpretive (combining signs with human insight), and intuitive (relying on inner gifts) methods.

Mysticism:

Mysticism is the pursuit of a direct, personal experience with the divine reality, often through spiritual practices like meditation, prayer, and contemplation. It emphasizes inner, intuitive knowledge over dogma or ordinary sensory perception. Mysticism is found across many religious and philosophical traditions, including Hinduism, Buddhism, Judaism, and Christianity.

Occult Activities encompass a wide range of practices and beliefs that explore the supernatural aspects

of reality. These activities often involve occult knowledge, rituals, ceremonies, and mystical experiences. These practices are outside the realm of organized religion and science. They may include divination, magic, alchemy, and communication with demons.

If you have knowingly or unknowingly been involved with any of these activities, such as the Eight Ball, the Ouija Board, Dream Catchers, Fortune Telling, Tarot Cards and books, music, art, and jewelry that have satanic or pagan idols on them.

"Heavenly Father, I come to You in the name of Jesus Christ. I confess that I have participated in occult practices, and I ask for Your forgiveness. I renounce and forsake all involvement in witchcraft, sorcery, divination, and seeking power or knowledge from any source other than You. I renounce my involvement and ask that any spiritual ties to these practices be broken. I confess my sin and ask You to cleanse me with the blood of Jesus. Fill me with Your Holy Spirit and lead me. I ask for Your protection over my life and my family. In Jesus' name, Amen".

Unholy Oaths, Vows, Pledges, Ceremonies in which you have participated. All of these refer to a promise of a sinful or harmful nature made to a person, group, or organization. This includes any ceremony and demon itself. This is a serious matter in our relationship with God. Repentance and seeking forgiveness from God are crucial steps in addressing such actions.

"Father, forgive me for participating in any oath, vow, pledge, or ceremony that is not of you." Amen

Cults

A group of people with a particular and often dangerously fanatical ideology. A cult has a leader who is either worshipped or greatly revered by the cult's followers. Cult leaders are charismatic, highly convincing, and good at getting people to listen to them. They build their image on lies, just as Satan does. Cult members follow one person or one belief system that can engage in a number of dangerous practices. Some cults emphasize self-improvement and the belief that all humans will ultimately be reconciled with God, regardless of their actions or beliefs in life. Cults clash with Christian doctrines of salvation through faith in Jesus and the Bible's teachings on the one true God.

"Father, forgive me for participating in any cult or group that does not worship you and accept Christ as their Lord and Savior. Amen"

Deliverance Ministry

The Bible emphasizes God's role as Deliverer, offering freedom from bondage and oppression, physically, emotionally, mentally, and spiritually, through faith in Jesus Christ. While not called "deliverance ministry," the Bible demonstrates Jesus's power to cast out demons, to break spiritual strongholds, and to comfort the people. This is a core belief of this ministry

God rescues you from various forms of oppression and bondage, such as demons and Spiritual Strongholds, which hinder spiritual growth and obedience to God. One way this is done is through the Deliverance Ministry. Through the power of Jesus Christ, this spiritual healing is available to each of us, as shown in Jesus's ministry and throughout the ages. Jesus, through His teachings and actions, emphasized deliverance from sin, spiritual bondage, physical afflictions, and the power of darkness. Deliverance offers freedom and healing through the love of God, faith in Jesus Christ, and the Power of the Holy Spirit.

Deliverance Ministry generally refers to being set free from demonic influence through the name of Jesus Christ, and with the gifts of the Holy Spirit you received at Baptism. It is designed to cast out demons, which allows you to overcome spiritual strongholds, such as negative behaviors, feelings, emotions, and experiences. It also helps to bring freedom to you, as you grow closer to God, and to minister to others in a better way. Deliverance Ministry is here to help you throw off demonic influences, so that you move forward to receive the life God intends for you to have.

Deliverance Ministry believes that baptized Christians, who profess they are believers in Christ, cannot be demonically possessed but can be oppressed by demons. This means baptized Christians can be influenced and persuaded mentally, physically, and emotionally by demons, which can cause them to move further away from God. The good news is that Baptized Christians have the ability to be helped and guided by the Holy Spirit, who is living within them. Through the gift of the Holy Spirit and the power of Jesus Christ, you can more easily and thoroughly receive a good result from the Deliverance Ministry. This allows you to take a new and closer step of faith in your journey with Jesus, your Lord and Savior.

As an unbaptized person who does not have the Holy Spirit living within you, demons have the ability to oppress your life in such a manner that they can affect you mentally, physically, emotionally, and spiritually. If you have not been baptized and have not accepted Jesus as their Lord and Savior, you can be possessed by demons. Possession means that demons have the ability to actually take over your life physically, emotionally, mentally, and spiritually. Unbelievers do not have the same help from Jesus Christ and the Holy Spirit as baptized Christians do. Because you have not accepted Jesus as your Lord and Savior and have not been baptized, you will find it to be much harder to achieve a complete Deliverance.

Deliverance Ministry is designed to help guide you through expressions of faith such as repentance and forgiveness. Also breaking generational curses, soul ties, and more. It guides you through the process as demons are cast out, generational curses are broken, and more. Deliverance offers you the opportunity for a new relationship with God, family, and friends.

Note: Unfortunately, not all Deliverance Ministries are the same. Some are untrained, some are only interested in the money they charge, some really do not have your best interest at heart, and some just make it up as they go along.

Other Deliverance Ministers see this as a ministry dedicated to God and committed to helping those who are living in demonic bondage. As they follow methods and practices that have been used over the centuries of the Church, they are only interested in doing His will. God the Father, Jesus, and the Holy Spirit are the heart of their ministry. They depend on the Bible for guidance. Helping others find freedom is most important to them. When you choose a Deliverance Ministry, it is wise to get counsel from your Pastor and others who have experienced deliverance.

Note: Deliverance Ministry is different from Healing Ministry. Healing ministry primarily refers to the restoration of the physical, emotional, and spiritual body through prayer and intercession. Deliverance Ministry refers to the casting out of demons in the Name of Jesus Christ, the love of God, and the help of the Holy Spirit. Deliverance Ministry can help set people free from torment, bondage, and oppression, as God the Father exhibits His steadfast love and protection. Deliverance is not a power encounter; it is a faith and love encounter. Jesus's love extended to you, and your love and worship given to Him.

Jesus As The Deliverer

Jesus Christ, the ultimate deliverer, rescues you from the spiritual bondage of sin and death through His death and resurrection. He delivers you from bondage. "The LORD is my rock and my fortress and my deliverer; My God, my strength, in whom I will trust; My shield and the horn of my salvation, my stronghold." *(Psalm 18:2).*

Authority in Jesus's Name

The New Testament emphasizes the authority given to believers in Jesus's name, including the power to cast out demons and to heal.

Jesus Deliverance from Sin and Bondage

Jesus came to preach the Gospel of the Kingdom of God, to perform miracles, such as healing the sick and brokenhearted, raising the dead, and setting the captives of Satan free. Highlighting His role as the Deliverer, Jesus came to offer Himself as a sacrifice for the sins of humanity, so that we can achieve salvation.

Power of the Holy Spirit

Jesus empowers believers to cast out demons and to overcome negative influences through the power of the Holy Spirit.

Repentance and Alignment with God

Jesus consistently invites repentance for experiencing true freedom, emphasizing that deliverance involves choosing to turn away from sin and align with God's will.

Faith in Jesus Christ

Jesus emphasizes that through faith in Him, believers can experience deliverance and walk in the freedom that only God can provide.

Signs of Belief

Jesus states that those who believe in Him will experience signs such as casting out demons, speaking in new tongues, and laying hands on the sick for healing. Also, receiving spiritual gifts, which are blessings or abilities given by God to help believers serve others.

Resisting the Devil

Jesus's teachings encourage believers to resist the devil and submit to God, emphasizing that through faith in Jesus and reliance on God's word, believers can experience deliverance.

Jesus as the Ultimate Deliverer

Jesus is presented as the ultimate deliverer who sets people free from sin, bondage, and spiritual oppression.

Freedom in Christ

Jesus's sacrifice on the cross is seen as the ultimate act of deliverance, freeing people from the penalty of sin and the power of darkness.

Deliverance from Eternal Punishment

Jesus rescues us from the "wrath to come" and offers eternal life to those who believe in Him.

Why Do People Come to Deliverance?

Many people come to Deliverance because they are seeking a way to be rescued from evil. They have turned to God, Jesus, and the Holy Spirit for help. When Jesus taught us how to pray at the end of the Lord's Prayer, He says "...and deliver us from evil." Some people come because of their belief that God can deliver them from evil. Other people come to deliverance ministries because they are tired of suffering from mental, physical, and spiritual oppression. They want freedom from evil demonic influence for their mind, body, emotion, and spirit. They have come to the conclusion that only God can help them overcome what is influencing their thinking, actions, and emotions.

They come to:

Remove hindrances:

Some believe that demonic influence can create hindrances in life, such as lust of the flesh, pride of life, and other temptations, which can impede a person's walk with God and their purpose in Christ. Deliverance is sought to break these bonds and overcome these obstacles.

Destroy the works of the enemy:

Deliverance ministry participants believe that Satan and his demons are actively working to steal, kill, and destroy. They seek deliverance to combat these forces through Jesus Christ.

Experience total deliverance in body, soul, mind, and spirit:

Deliverance is pursued to address the brokenness and effects of sin on a person's life, including physical ailments, emotional struggles, unclean thinking, and sinful patterns. Deliverance can lead to freedom from these issues and empower individuals to live according to God's will.

Overcome the effects of generational curses:

Some traditions associate persistent problems like poverty, addiction, or illness with curses passed down through generations due to ancestral sins. Deliverance practices include confessing and repenting for the sins of your ancestors to break these curses and their negative impact.

Heal from trauma and victimization:

Traumatic experiences can create openings for demonic spirits, leading to issues like fear, insecurity, or bitterness. Individuals may seek deliverance to find healing from these wounds and break free from the resulting emotional and spiritual bondage.

Break free from the bondage of long-term sin:

When individuals struggle with persistent sin patterns and rebellion against God, some believe that deliverance is necessary to break the demonic hold that may be enabling those behaviors.

It is important to note that the concept and practice of deliverance ministry are not universally accepted within Christianity. Some denominations and theologians express concerns about its methodology and interpretations of scripture. However, for those who believe in its principles, deliverance represents a path toward spiritual freedom, healing, and a deeper relationship with God.

Process of Deliverance

It is important for you to know that many ministries use different techniques and strategies to drive out demons. Some are very successful and some are not. Basically, during a Deliverance Session trained Deliverance Ministers will guide and oversee your personal Deliverance experience.

It is very important that the Deliverance Minister you choose is trained and experienced. This always entails their going through Deliverance themselves. They also participate in ongoing Deliverance education, such as books, media presentations, and seminars. They participate in an apprenticeship program, which lasts at least six months to one year. In truth, Deliverance Ministry training is ongoing. They have great faith in the power of Jesus Christ, the guidance and comfort of the Holy Spirit, and the unrelenting love of God the Father.

Deliverance Ministers are committed to your safety and well-being. It is the responsibility of a trained and experienced lead Deliverance minister to guide the process. The lead minister has had years of Deliverance Experience. The other Deliverance Ministers always follow the lead minister during the Deliverance. It is through the power of Jesus Christ that the Deliverance ministers take charge of the demons, command all demons to repair any damage they have caused, and to leave and go immediately and directly to the abyss. They act on the belief that through the power of Jesus Christ, all demons will be cast out.

Prior to the Deliverance Session, this open-ended question is asked: "Why did you come to Deliverance? This question can provide the Deliverance Minister the opportunity to listen intently to their responses. Many times, their responses will help identify potential demons, determine areas of concern, and learn more about their needs. Everyone who comes to Deliverance is different.

Unforgiveness

In order for the Deliverance Session to be successful, there can be NO unforgiveness in your life. Unforgiveness is legal permission for demons to torment believers.

The Parable of the Unmerciful Servant:

Jesus tells a parable where a servant who refuses to forgive a small debt is thrown into "prison to be tormented" until he pays his entire debt. This is interpreted as a metaphor for how unforgiveness can put a person into a spiritual prison and grant demons a legal right to torment them. *(Matthew 18:23-35).*

- Forgiveness is the key to this process.
- Forgiveness is not about forgetting or condoning.
- Forgiveness is about giving the person who hurt you the gift of grace. The same grace that Jesus gave you from the Cross.
- Forgiveness is a holy and sacrificial act.

In the Bible, forgiveness is a central theme, both God forgiving people for their sins through Christ's sacrifice, and people being commanded to forgive one another as a condition for receiving God's forgiveness. "For if you forgive men their trespasses, your heavenly Father will also forgive you. But if you do not forgive men their trespasses, neither will your Father forgive your trespasses". *(Matthew 6:14-15)*

Forgiveness emphasizes the importance of releasing resentment and showing kindness, compassion, and mercy, as you model the forgiveness shown to you by God. "Bear with each other and forgive one another if any of you has a grievance against someone. Forgive as the Lord forgave you." *(Colossians 3:13).*

Forgiveness is not Condoning

- Forgiveness does not excuse, approve of, or justify the harmful actions of another person. It is a personal choice to release your anger, resentment, and the emotional burden of your past hurts.
- Forgiveness helps you to reclaim your own peace of mind and begin the process of healing.
- Forgiveness can occur without reconciliation and does not imply that consequences for the offender are unnecessary.

Personal Forgiveness Prayer

"Father, because You have forgiven me, I choose to forgive others, everyone who has hurt me, lied to me or disappointed me, I forgive. I confess unforgiveness as sin and repent of it. I receive Your forgiveness and apply it to my life by forgiving others and myself. Thank You Lord, for Your grace and mercy, in Jesus' Name. Amen."

Forgiveness

You now have the opportunity to forgive everyone in your life who has hurt you, betrayed you, caused you pain, or even just made you feel bad. Any negative action directed at you. This includes very small to very large negative actions or speech directed at you. Any action that made you feel bad,

Recalling one person at a time say:

I choose to forgive _____.

If you do not remember their name, just say "that person". You know who that person is, and so does God, so it is not necessary to remember their name.

Occult Involvement Prayer

If there was ever any involvement, however innocent, in Satanic activities, witchcraft, cults, or occult activities, they must be renounced.

Prayer

"Father, I renounce any bond or agreement I ever made with Satan and the kingdom of darkness. I know there can be no valid contract with a liar, and I renounce any words, oaths, or pledges made to Satan, and I choose to be totally free from them. I choose to be cleansed from any ties with Satan in Jesus' Name, Amen."

Personal Repentance

Repent of Personal Sin

To repent of personal sin, pray to God, and confess your sin. Then express sincere regret and sorrow for your offense against Him. Resolve to change your behavior as you turn away from sin. Ask for God's forgiveness through Jesus Christ and seek His help to live a righteous life

Prayer

"Merciful Father in heaven,

I come before You today with a truly repentant heart, acknowledging my sins and shortcomings.

I confess that I have sinned against You by (mention sins here). I know that these actions have created distance between me and You, and I am truly sorry for them. I believe Your Son, Jesus Christ, died for my sins and rose from the dead. I am turning away from these sinful ways and choosing to follow Him. Please forgive me for my sins, Lord Jesus. Create in me a pure heart. I give You my whole heart and life, asking that You come into it and be my Lord and Savior.

Thank you for Your unfailing love and abundant mercy. I rely on Your grace to restore and renew me, and to help me turn away from temptation and live according to Your will. Amen"

Repentance

Repentance is a central concept in Christianity. It is often considered a spiritual cleansing. It is a process that includes sorrow for sin, a change of mind about sin and Christ, and a turning from sin toward God.

Repentance is the act of regretting your past wrongdoing and committing to change for the better. This change of mind involves turning away from sin and towards God, often accompanied by sorrow, a desire for forgiveness, and a commitment to altered behavior. While it includes feeling remorse, genuine repentance also implies a firm resolve to change your actions and direction in life.

Repentance is a precursor to freedom from bondage and demonic oppression. You cannot wait for God to deliver you, while God is waiting for you to repent. Some people are waiting for God to deliver them, while God is waiting for them to repent. To be delivered from the power of sin, oppression, and demons, you must come into complete agreement with God. You cannot minimize sin in any way. You must own up to sin and repent. "Therefore submit to God. Resist the devil and he will flee from you." *(James 4:7)*.

Generational Curses

It is through the Father and Mother's bloodline that negative traits, behaviors, or experiences are passed down from one generation to the next, impacting the lives of subsequent family members.

A generational curse refers to the idea of recurring patterns of misfortune, sin, or suffering that are transmitted through family lines from the sins of ancestors. These patterns can manifest as chronic illnesses, addiction, financial hardship, abuse, and repeated negative behaviors. While some biblical interpretations suggest divine punishment extends for a few generations, other interpretations, particularly under the New Covenant, emphasize individual responsibility for sin and offer freedom from such cycles through faith and grace.

Biblical Basis:

The concept has roots in Old Testament passages, such as *(Exodus 34:7)* and *(Deuteronomy 5:9)*, which speak of God punishing the sins of fathers on their children to the third or fourth generation.

Behavioral & Spiritual Patterns:

These "curses" are often seen as recurring spiritual or behavioral patterns, such as addiction, idolatry, rebellion, and negative feelings, transmitted through family lines.

Breaking the Cycle:

For Christians, this often involves spiritual warfare, prayer, and aligning with divine principles to break the cycle, focusing on God's grace and a believer's individual freedom from curses under the New Covenant, as described in *Ezekiel 18*, which states individuals are responsible for their own sins.

Breaking Generational Curses

First, make a list of the sins of the Father's Blood Line and the sins of the Mother's Blood Line.

Father I repent for the sins of Father's Blood Line (list sins here) _____.

I break every oath, every vow, every pledge, every ceremony, and blood sacrifice that was done through witchcraft and any other occult ritual. I renounce it now and put it under the blood of Jesus.

Father I repent for the sins of Mother's Blood Line (list sins here) _____.

I break every oath, every vow, every pledge, every ceremony, and blood sacrifice that was done through witchcraft and any other occult ritual. I renounce it now and put it under the blood of Jesus.

Involvement in the Occult

Any involvement in demonic activity, no matter how innocent, such as satanic activities, witchcraft, cults, or occult activities, must be renounced.

Repeat after me:

Father I repent of and renounce any oath, vow, covenant or agreement I have made to _____ . I renounce it all now and put it under the blood of Satan.

Applies to both your Father's Bloodline and your Mother's Bloodline.

Personal Sin

In the Bible, personal sin is defined as any thought, word, or action that goes against God's perfect standard of holiness. It stems from an individual's own will. It encompasses both sins of commission (doing what one should not do) and sins of omission (failing to do what one should do).

While the Bible acknowledges that "all have sinned and fall short of the glory of God" *(Romans 3:23)*, it emphasizes individual responsibility for your sins, requiring personal repentance and faith in Christ for forgiveness and reconciliation with God.

Being delivered from personal sin is the process of being set free from the power and bondage of Satan. Through faith in Jesus Christ, you can acknowledge your inability to overcome sin on your own. You can believe that through Christ's death on the cross, He broke sin's power over you. Through Christ, you are enabled to live a life of holiness.

Soul Ties

A demonic soul tie can be formed when two individuals share a profound emotional or spiritual connection that causes negative responses. Recognize that this type of soul tie is negative, causing unhealthy emotional bonds, codependency, or exhaustion. Sometimes they can be very harmful, so it is important to break the Soul Ties that hurt us.

Breaking Soul Ties

To break a soul tie, you must acknowledge its negative nature, repent for any sinful acts that formed it, and then verbally renounce and break the spiritual connection through prayer, often in the name of Jesus Christ. You must also commit to forgiving the other person, setting boundaries, seeking support from godly counsel, and inviting the Holy Spirit to fill the void with peace and God's presence.

"Through the name of Jesus Christ I break every soul tie and ever unholy bond with _____ I give back what I took from _____ and take back what I gave to _____."

Say out loud as you put in the person's first name. If you do not remember their name just say "that person".

Breaking Soul ties involving sexual relationships outside of marriage.

Each occurrence can be an entry point for demons. To break this type of Soul Tie, you must confess each episode as sin and choose to be free from each one.

Repent for sex relationships outside of marriage:

"Father, I confess the sin of sexual relations outside of marriage. I renounce my sinful activity in Jesus' Name. I ask for Your forgiveness for my sins." Amen.

Breaking Soul Ties

"Through the name of Jesus Christ I break every soul tie and ever unholy bond with _____ I give back what I took from _____ and take back what I gave to _____."

Demonic Legal Rights

The concept of demons having "legal rights" is not explicitly found in the Bible but is interpreted from some passages. To "break demonic legal rights," you can use biblical principles to renounce known sins, forgive others, break agreements with the occult, and claim Christ's victory over evil. This involves repentance, renunciation of past actions like unforgiveness or involvement in the occult, and prayer to declare freedom in Jesus' name.

Biblical Basis for "Legal Rights"

"In your anger do not sin. Do not let the sun go down while you are still angry, and do not give the devil a foothold." *(Ephesians 4:26-27)*.

"And having disarmed the powers and authorities, he made a public spectacle of them, triumphing over them by the cross." *(Colossians 2:15)*.

How to Break Demonic "Legal Rights"

Repent of Known Sins:

Confess and repent of any known sins that might give a demon legal grounds to stay.

Forgive Others:

Release unforgiveness toward those who have wronged you, which can be a basis for demonic torment.

Renounce Occult Involvement:

Get rid of cursed objects and renounce any involvement in witchcraft, sorcery, or false religions.

Claim Christ's Authority:

Recognize that Jesus Christ purchased you with His blood, giving Him alone the legal right to you. You are redeemed and belong to God.

Pray Aloud:

Declare your freedom and break the agreement with demonic influences by praying and speaking your freedom out loud.

Break Demonic Curses:

Some traditions teach that generational curses, stemming from ancestral sins, can give demons legal rights, and these can be broken through prayer and repentance.

Repent of Satanic Activities

To repent of satanic activities, you need to confess your involvement as sin, renounce all association with the occult and Satan. In the name of Jesus Christ, ask for God's forgiveness with a sincere heart and commitment to follow His word. Remove all demonic objects, seek supportive spiritual fellowship, and replace negative influences with God's truth by means of The Bible and prayer.

Steps to Repentance:

Confess Your Sins:

Honestly admit to God that you participated in these activities and acknowledge them as sin.

Renounce the Activity:

Formally reject and disown any connection to satanic practices and the devil.

Ask for Forgiveness:

Ask God to forgive you and wash you clean through the power of Jesus Christ's blood.

Turn to God:

Make a complete 180-degree turn in your life, moving away from sin and toward God.

Remove Demonic Objects:

Dispose of any physical items used for occult practices or that are symbols of the occult.

Seek Freedom:

Protect yourself from any demonic spirits or influences that may regain entry through sin.

Traumatic Life Event

A traumatic event is a deeply distressing or overwhelming experience that can cause significant psychological and emotional harm. It is typically characterized by the following features:

Intense Fear or Helplessness. The event poses a real or perceived threat to a person's life or physical safety.

It is important to note that what constitutes a traumatic event can vary from person to person, depending on individual experiences, beliefs, and cultural background.

This event can include witnessing or being a victim of violence, or experiencing a sudden and unexpected loss. Most often, it is experienced as a type of physical, mental, or sexual abuse. Traumatic life events impact us in negative ways. The experience of a traumatic event usually has a significant and lasting impact on your life, causing distress, disruption, or changes in behavior or coping mechanisms. To be totally free from this abusive event and negative memory, you must turn it over to God.

To find total freedom from these events, it is necessary to turn your negative thoughts and feelings over to God.

Ask these questions:

Close your eyes and think back to this traumatic event. Do you remember?

In most cases, the traumatic event is remembered, and the person sees or feels what Jesus is doing during the event. This gives you an opportunity to see that Jesus loves you in all circumstances and He is there with you during bad times in your life.

Can you see Jesus there? What is He doing? What is He saying?

Jesus is always there to comfort, protect, and love you.

Remember, Jesus is always there with you, in the best of times and in the worst of times. You are a child of God, and He loves and cares for you more than you can ever imagine. He will never leave you, and He will never forsake you. He is with you even until the end of time.

Casting Out Demons

Deliverance is a religious and spiritual practice of evicting demons from you or an area believed to be oppressed or possessed by them. It is expelling demonic spirits from a person, place, or thing. In Christianity, this is done by invoking the name of Jesus Christ, who gave His disciples the power to cast out demons in His holy name. The practice involves prayers, specific commands to the demons, and a reliance on faith and Divine power.

The goal is to restore individuals to health and wholeness. Through faith in Jesus Christ, casting out demons is used to liberate you from the influence of evil, sin, and demonic oppression. This includes freedom from demonic control over your mind, body, and emotions. Also, casting out demons demonstrates Jesus' authority over spiritual forces. Christian believers view Deliverance as a compassionate act of healing and liberation, rather than a punishment for the oppressed or possessed person.

Biblical Basis for Authority:

Jesus Gives Authority:

Jesus directly gave His disciples authority to drive out demons and heal the sick *(Matthew 10:1, Luke 9:1)*.

Delegated power to the disciples:

Jesus explicitly gave his twelve disciples "authority over unclean spirits, to cast them out, and to heal every disease and every affliction" *(Matthew 10:1, Mark 3:15, Luke 9:1)*. He later extended this authority to 72 other followers who returned with joy, reporting that "even the demons are subject to us in your name" *(Luke 10:1, 17)*.

Authority for all believers:

In his final words before ascending to heaven, Jesus promised that casting out demons "in my name" would be one of the signs accompanying those who believe in him *(Mark 16:17)*. The book of

Acts provides examples of this, such as when the Apostle Paul commanded a spirit of divination to leave a slave girl, and it did. *(Acts 16:16–18)*.

The greater power of the Holy Spirit:

The Apostle John emphasizes that the power residing in believers is superior to the power of evil spirits. "You, dear children, are from God and have overcome them, because the one who is in you is greater than the one who is in the world" *(1 John 4:4)*. The power to cast out demons is understood by some to come from living under the influence and power of the Holy Spirit. *(Acts 1:8)*.

Commissioning of Disciples:

He also commissioned the seventy-two to cast out demons in His name. *(Luke 10:17-20)*

Authority in the Name of Jesus:

As followers of Jesus and believers in His name, Christians are given authority to operate under His Lordship to cast out demons. *(Mark 16:17, Luke 10:19)*.

Key aspects of the Christian belief include:

Christian perspective:

In Christianity, the practice is primarily associated with the ministry of Jesus, who demonstrated authority over evil forces by frequently casting out demons from afflicted people. Believers hold that this authority was passed on to his disciples and continues through the power of the Holy Spirit.

Source of authority:

Christians believe that a demon's power is no match for the Holy Spirit dwelling within a believer. They declare the name of Jesus to command a demon to leave, because Jesus' name is considered to be above every other name.

Signs of oppression and possession:

Depending on the denomination, symptoms believed to signal demonic possession can include supernatural strength, speaking in unknown languages, having secret knowledge, aversion to sacred objects, personality change, violent outbursts, intrusive thoughts, and connection to the occult. Some physical signs are superhuman strength, unexplained physical phenomena, physical afflictions, and attacks during sleep.

Method Involved in Deliverance:

Verbal commands:

Directly commanding and using authoritative language as you tell the demons to leave in the name of Jesus Christ, to bind all of the demons together, and to repair all of their damage before it leaves.

Repentance and Renunciation:

Acknowledging and rejecting the works of the devil and renouncing the demon's influence.

Faith and Prayer:

Relying on the name of Jesus Christ, the power of the Holy Spirit, and a strong faith in God.

Key Instances of Jesus Casting Out Demons

A Man in the Capernaum Synagogue:

Jesus casts a "spirit of an unclean demon" out of a man in the synagogue, commanding it to leave him. *(Mark 1:23)*.

The Gerasene Demoniac:

Jesus encounters a man possessed by a "legion" of demons. He commands the spirits to leave the man and enter a herd of pigs, which then rush into the sea *(Matthew 8, Mark 5:1-20, and Luke 8:26-39)*.

The Boy with Epilepsy:

Jesus casts out a deaf and mute spirit that caused a boy to have convulsions and fall into fire or water. *(Matthew 17:14-16, Mark 9:14-29, and Luke 9:37-43).*

A Blind and Mute Man:

Jesus heals a man who was possessed by a demon and simultaneously blind and unable to speak. *(Matthew 12:22-23 and Luke 11:14).*

Mary Magdalene:

It is mentioned that Jesus first appeared to Mary Magdalene after his resurrection, having previously cast out seven demons from her. *(Mark 16:9-10).*

The Syrophoenician Woman's Daughter:

While not a direct casting out, Jesus heals the daughter of a Syrophoenician woman who was oppressed by a demon, acknowledging the woman's great faith. *(Mark 7:24-29).*

Casting Out Demons in Dreams

Experiencing demonic dreams has spiritual and religious meaning. Scientific perspectives often explain these dreams as extreme manifestations of anxiety, stress, or unresolved psychological issues. Response to these dreams varies, with religious individuals often turning to prayer and spiritual warfare.

Christians interpret demonic dreams as a manifestation of spiritual warfare or acknowledgment of areas requiring deliverance. Some believe it signifies that their spiritual eyes are being opened to the ongoing battle against demonic forces. If such dreams are recurring or causing distress, seek spiritual counsel and guidance from mature believers, Pastors, or Deliverance Ministers can be helpful.

A demonic dream is a nightmare characterized by vivid imagery of threatening figures or forces, feelings of spiritual oppression, and a sense of unease. Psychologically, these dreams may stem from stress, trauma, or anxiety, which the subconscious processes through nightmares. From a spiritual perspective, they are seen as attacks from malevolent entities and can involve feeling paralyzed or choked upon waking.

Bible verses about casting out demons in sleep:

While the Bible speaks about spiritual warfare and casting out demons in general, there is not a specific passage that directly addresses casting out demons in your sleep, neither dream nor nightmare. However, biblical principles and verses relate to spiritual authority, protection, and God's power over evil. These can be applied to demonic encounters in dreams.

Authority of Believers:

Jesus gave believers authority over demons. "Behold, I have given you authority to tread on serpents and scorpions, and over all the power of the enemy, and nothing shall hurt you". *(Luke 10:19)*. One can use the name and authority of Jesus to resist and command demonic forces to leave, even in dreams.

Trust in God's Protection:

The Bible encourages trust in God's protection, especially at night., "You shall not be afraid of the terror by night, nor of the arrow that flies by day." *(Psalm 91:5-6).*

"When you lie down, you will not be afraid; when you lie down, your sleep will be sweet". *(Proverbs 3:24 states).*

The Power of Prayer:

Prayer is a powerful weapon against spiritual attacks. "Do not be anxious about anything, but in everything, by prayer and petition, with thanksgiving, present your requests to God. And the peace of God, which transcends all understanding, will guard your hearts and your minds in Christ Jesus". *(Philippians 4:6–7)* says Prayer before sleep can establish a spiritual protection.

The Armor of God:

The Bible encourages believers to "take up the whole armor of God, that you may be able to withstand in the evil day, and having done all, to stand firm". This spiritual armor includes truth, righteousness, the gospel of peace, faith, salvation, the Word of God, and prayer. Applying these principles, even mentally or spiritually in a dream, can be a way to stand against demonic influence. *(Ephesians 6:13).*

Getting ready for Sleep:

Before going to sleep, you can start with a prayer of protection and ask for spiritual covering during the night.

"Heavenly Father, I come before You, seeking Your divine protection over my life. Surround me with Your angels and shield me from every harm and danger. Let no evil come near me or my loved ones, for You are my refuge and fortress. I trust in Your mighty power to guard and keep me safe, now and always, Amen."

It is also important to prepare your mind for sleep by avoiding ungodly influences. Fill your thoughts with Godly things like scripture, prayer, and worship music. Avoid ungodly influences, create a peaceful environment, and commit your night to God.

Should you have a demonic dream or dreams, you can rebuke the demon in the name of Jesus.

You can declare victory and spiritual authority as you use scripture, pray for protection, and spiritual covering.

"Heavenly Father, I commit my mind, body, and spirit into Your hands tonight. I plead the blood of Jesus over my dreams and rebuke every demonic attack. Surround me with Your angels and let Your peace guard my heart and mind. In Jesus' name, Amen."

Some practical steps you can take include confessing sin, blessing your bedroom, and avoiding harmful content before sleep. For consistent help, maintain a spiritual life of prayer and worship, and if the issue persists, seek prayer or counseling from a spiritual leader.

Actions you can take after a dream:

Pray and Seek Discernment.

Ask God for insight into why you are having these dreams and what he wants you to learn from them.

Rebuke the enemy:

Upon waking up from a demonic or evil dream, you need to immediately rebuke the enemy out loud in the name of Jesus.

"Almighty God, Who delivered Your people from the bondage of the adversary, and through Your Son cast down Satan like lightning, deliver me also from every influence of unclean spirits. Command

Satan to depart far from me by the power of Your only begotten Son. Rescue me from demonic imaginings and darkness." Amen.

Pray for protection:

Use prayers for protection and invoke the authority of Christ over any spiritual attacks against you or your family.

"Lord Jesus, thank You for the authority You have given me over the power of the enemy. I bind every demonic spirit attempting to attack me in my dreams and cast them into the abyss. I declare freedom and peace over my sleep. In Jesus' name, Amen."

Address potential entry points.

It is believed that unaddressed sins, unforgiveness, or exposure to occult items can open doors to spiritual attacks. After you destroy occult items in your home, you can repent and ask for forgiveness for your sins, your unforgiveness, and allowing occult items into your home. If the demonic attack reoccurs, it is wise to seek out the Deliverance Ministry for further help.

Consult a spiritual leader:

If the dreams are persistent, frightening, or confusing, it can be helpful to seek guidance from a trusted spiritual leader, counselor, or Deliverance Minister.

Journaling:

Write down the details of the dream and pray, and listen for God's guidance.

A Word to the Wise

Deliverance ministry can go wrong in several ways. Some ministers lack the proper training or developed gifts of discernment, prophecy, and wisdom. This can lead to incorrect diagnosis of issues or ineffective techniques. Others might prioritize theatrics over genuine care, potentially causing emotional harm or spiritual confusion. Furthermore, some ministers may lack accountability, training, or fail to provide adequate follow-up care, leaving individuals vulnerable after the deliverance session.

These are potential pitfalls:

Lack of Training and Discernment:

Some individuals may attempt Deliverance Ministry without adequate theological understanding, training, or practical experience. This will lead to misidentification of issues and inappropriate application of techniques used in Deliverance Ministry. Training or an apprenticeship, led by a qualified Deliverance Minister, is critical. The Deliverance Minister is constantly turning to God for ongoing direction, wisdom, insight, experience, and commitment to the people who come for help. This is a ministry directed by God and empowered by the Holy Spirit. All authority comes from Jesus. A deliverance minister is the servant of God who lives in humility and faith.

Lack of Accountability:

Some Deliverance Ministries operate without proper oversight or accountability structures, making them susceptible to abuse of power and unethical practices.

Lack of Follow-up:

The people who come to Deliverance Ministry should be followed by ongoing support and guidance from their Deliverance Ministers. Without proper follow-up, individuals may relapse or struggle to integrate what they have learned to sustain their freedom.

Lack of Training:

Ministers may lack proper understanding or knowledge of mental health conditions and trauma, potentially misdiagnosing and harming vulnerable individuals. No Deliverance Minister should diagnose any individual without a degree in the mental health field. Deliverance is not a therapy session. It is an opportunity for Jesus to cast out demons and heal the person. Deliverance Ministers are disciples of Jesus committed to listening to Jesus and serving God. They are not therapist.

Misdiagnosis:

Not all problems are caused by demonic influence. Deliverance ministry can be misused to address psychological or emotional issues that require professional counseling or medical treatment.

Focus on Self instead of Care:

Some ministers may use Deliverance as a means to attract attention or build their own reputation, rather than focusing on the genuine needs of the individual.

Emotional Harm:

Intense emotional reactions can occur during deliverance, and if not handled with care and sensitivity, this can lead to emotional distress or trauma. A trained and experienced Deliverance Minister has been taught how to deal with spiritual trauma.

Negative Impact on Mental Health:

If deliverance is used instead of or in addition to professional mental health treatment, it can be harmful. If the person is being treated for any psychosis, their doctor needs to approve their attendance at a Delivery Session.

Spiritual Confusion:

If deliverance is not handled biblically, it can lead to confusion about God's character, His power, and the nature of spiritual warfare. Therefore, it is necessary for each Deliverance Minister to constantly spend time in and study the Bible and in prayer with God, for the purpose of knowing Him better.

Misinterpretations and Unbiblical Practices:

Misinterpretations of the Bible can lead to significant errors in understanding and practicing Christian faith. These misinterpretations can stem from various factors, including a lack of knowledge, resistance to the truth, and the influence of false teachers. To avoid misinterpretations, it is crucial to consider the historical and cultural context and rely on the Holy Spirit for Guidance. Therefore, it is critical that Deliverance Ministers research the historical and cultural context as they read the Bible for guidance. Their goal is to better know and understand God's message through scripture.

Excessive Focus on Demons:

Some ministries may place an undue emphasis on demonic activity. They attribute various issues, including mental health struggles, to demonic influence, rather than acknowledging other potential factors. Therefore, an interview is always important so that the person's story is shared. This provides an opportunity to determine if Deliverance would be helpful to them.

Fabricated Rituals:

Some Deliverance practices may rely on man-made rituals, renunciations, or inner healing models that are not supported by Scripture. Therefore, the Deliverance Ministers are relying on their own means and not on God's. Through the name of Jesus Christ, people are delivered from Demonic Oppression and Possession. Deliverance Ministers can do nothing by themselves. The

Deliverance Minister understands that he or she is an instrument of God, and without Him there is no Deliverance.

Twisting Scripture:

Some Ministers take Scripture out of context or misinterpret passages to support doctrines like the "spiritual spouse" or "night demon", which cause all emotional and psychological problems. They focus on the ritual instead of Christ and the person wanting to be delivered. Obsessive focus on demons and spiritual warfare, as well as dependence on specific teachers or leaders of Deliverance, fosters fear and dependence on the ministry.

Learning from Demons:

Some Deliverance Ministers may engage in prolonged conversations or arguments with demons, seeking information from them, which is discouraged in scripture. A Deliverance Minister should never carry on a conversation with any demon. Casting out Demons is a partnership with Jesus; therefore, a Deliverance Minister does not need to have a conversation with the demon. Jesus refused to do it in the wilderness. We should refuse to do it wherever we are. In John 8, Jesus said he is a liar from the beginning, and behind that trickery is a murderous intent "In the synagogue there was a man possessed by a demon, an impure spirit. He cried out at the top of his voice, "Go away! What do you want with us, Jesus of Nazareth? Have you come to destroy us? I know who you are—the Holy One of God!" "Be quiet!" Jesus said sternly. "Come out of him!" Then the demon threw the man down before them all and came out without injuring him." *(Luke 4:33-35).*

Abusive and Manipulative Practices cause Spiritual abuse:

Deliverance ministry can become a tool for spiritual abuse, with ministers exerting excessive control over individuals, fostering dependency, and preying on a person's fears.

Exploitation and Financial Gain:

Some individuals may use Deliverance Ministry as a means of gaining popularity, personal benefit, or financial exploitation. Many Deliverance Ministers charge nothing, some only charge a small amount for expenses, and many only take donations if offered. Remember this is a ministry, not a job.

Neglecting professional help:

In some cases, individuals may be discouraged from seeking professional counseling or medical help for legitimate issues, being told that Deliverance is the only solution. This lie is actually extremely harmful to the person.

Psychological and Emotional Harm:

Deliverance sessions, particularly for those with past trauma or abuse, can trigger dissociative states or other negative reactions, potentially exacerbating their distress.

Increased Fear and Anxiety:

An overemphasis on the demonic can lead to excessive fear and anxiety, creating an unhealthy focus on demonic activity rather than a relationship with Christ. This can undermine a person's faith and assurance in the sufficiency of Christ's work, fostering a sense of bondage rather than freedom.

Ignoring Human Responsibility:

Placing all blame on demons can allow individuals to avoid taking responsibility for their own actions and choices, hindering personal growth and development.

In conclusion, while deliverance ministry aims to help individuals overcome negative spiritual influences, it carries inherent risks and can be harmful if not approached with proper biblical understanding, discernment, ethical guidelines, and a genuine concern for the well-being of those seeking help.

In Closing

A calling to Deliverance Ministry is often indicated by a strong desire to see people set free from spiritual bondage. A personal experience with Deliverance is a calling to enter into Spiritual Warfare and daily prayer and Bible reading. Through the power of Jesus Christ, the Deliverance minister's desire is to help others on their spiritual journey, as well as to pray and to serve God.

You may be drawn to learning about Deliverance, have seen demons in dreams or even at a young age, and may have experienced near-death experiences. Confirmation from spiritual mentors and the manifestation of spiritual gifts can also signal a calling to the Deliverance Ministry. It is important to remember that hearing and following a calling from God is part of your personal journey with Him. Seeking guidance from spiritual mentors and leaders is very important in understanding and confirming a call to Deliverance Ministry.

Should you be called to Deliverance Ministry, seek the best training you can find. Deliverance Ministry is an apprenticeship. It is not something you learn out of a book. It is a ministry that calls for a commitment to God and to His people. In deciding to become a Deliverance Minister, exercise discernment and pray to God for guidance. This ensures that the ministry you choose aligns with the will of God and sound biblical teaching. Through Jesus Christ, it offers you the opportunity to focus on the sufficiency of God's love and the guidance of the Holy Spirit. All of this promotes healthy spiritual growth and discipleship.

A good Deliverance Minister strives for these Spiritual Gifts and Talents: Faith, Healing, Prophecy, and Discernment. Encouragement, Word of Wisdom, Word of Knowledge, Mercy, Giving, Exhortation, Evangelism, and Service.

"Fear not, for I am with you even until the end of the age." Amen.

www.ingramcontent.com/pod-product-compliance
Lightning Source LLC
Chambersburg PA
CBHW041820090426

42811CB00009B/1044